Complete Meditation

Complete Meditation

By Steve Kravette
Illustrated by Plunkett Dodge

Para Research
Rockport, Massachusetts

Complete Meditation
by Steve Kravette

International Standard Book Number: 0-914918-28-1

Typeset in 14 point Bem on a Compugraphic Editwriter 7500
Printed by R.R. Donnelley & Sons Co.
on 55-pound Warren Sebago paper

Published by Para Research, Inc.
Whistlestop Mall
Rockport, Massachusetts 01966-1494

Manufactured in the United States of America

First Printing, January 1982, 5,000 copies

Dedication

With love,
this book is dedicated to
Edna,
Norma,
Carolyn,
and Jennifer,
for the profound spiritual experience
each has had upon my life.

Contents

Meditation and being

Meditation and being

Anyone can meditate.
Including you.
It's not a secret science
or a mystical esoteric process,
although you may have heard that it was.
And it doesn't involve a lot of discipline
or a lot of discomfort.
All it takes
is a little commitment,
a little practice,
and a little development
to learn to use this fundamental tool
for self-expansion and personal growth.

Meditation is easier
than walking across a meadow,
driving your car through traffic,
or cutting a peanut butter sandwich in half.

All those things
and everything else that you do
require an incredibly complex degree
of coordination
between mind and body.

Millions of neural, muscular, and cellular
connections
must be made and maintained.
And the degree of energy control
and precise channeling of your lifeforce
into action
is almost impossible to imagine.

Yet,
you've learned to do
everything that you do
almost automatically.

To meditate,
you don't have to learn to do anything.
You simply have to be.
In fact,
the whole idea
is to stop doing whatever you are already doing,
consciously or unconsciously,
and focus completely
on the subject of your meditation
in a relaxed, flowing, noncontrolling way.
Until you actually become it.
And it actually becomes you.

That's all complete meditation is.
It's the most natural thing in the world.
And you're no stranger to it.
You've already been meditating for years.
Although you may not have known
that was what you were doing.

For instance,
when you watch television
or hem a pair of slacks
or lose yourself
in a spontaneous race between two raindrops
down a windowpane,
you are meditating.
In each case,
you are immersed in a process
that takes you out of yourself
and your normal stream of consciousness
and beyond your ordinary sense of time.

The problem is,
what you meditate on
can profoundly influence, program, and direct
your energy, your life cycle,
and all the space around you.

So when you focus on a tv show
that's excessively violent, morbid, or vapid,
you end up
limp and fatigued.
When you focus on your breath,
a leaf, a stone, the jewel in your ring,
a sound or a positive thought,
you end the experience
more perceptive and more alert.
And when you focus on your own energy
and state of being,
you re-enter
completely refreshed, revitalized, and recharged.

In the beginning,
when you were a baby,
you spent all your time meditating
on your growth and development
and expansiveness.
That's why time
was so much more timeless then.
You were in a state of harmony
with the universe around you.
And when you needed something,
you knew just how to materialize it.

You began to lose your meditational harmony
as you began
to develop your sense of self,
which separated and differentiated
you
from everything else.

And you lost even more of it
as you developed a rational analytical ego,
which kept trying to find
logical ways to shield and protect you
from your inner sense
of alienation and dissociation
from everything else that is.
And which hooked you
into books, television, newspapers,
teachers, and other authorities
as the only way to gain
knowledge and understanding of your self
and your universe.

All of this came about
in a perfectly normal and natural way.
And it's all
a necessary part of the process
of growing up as a human
being.
But growing never stops.
And just because you've grown
to wherever you are right now,
it doesn't mean you're done.

There's more.
A whole lot more.
Just as trees grow continuously
and change with each passing season,
all cellular beings
grow continuously too.
Including you.

As far as creaturehood goes
on a physical level,
life ends when growth ends.

The point is,
now that you've grown
as separated from your universe as you are,
the next phase of growing
needs to include
reintegrating and reharmonizing yourself
with all that is
all around you.

Opening channels to that process,
gaining intutive knowledge
and inner understanding,
and creating expansiveness
out of anxiety and chaos
through complete meditation
are the results you can expect from this book.

Taking it a step further:
Meditation is the word
that describes your state of consciousness
when you have become
so totally immersed
in an object, an event, or a thought
that your level of awareness shifts
and you lose your sense of separateness
from that object, event, or thought.

You become
so completely involved and centered
in what and where you are
that your mental chatter fades away,
your body tension and emotional anxieties melt,
sensory distractions in your environment disappear,
and time flows at an altered rate of speed.

A cozy fireplace,
all aglow while snowflakes dance
and the wind whistles outside,
is a meditation.
As you watch the everchanging
hypnotic images within the flames,
you respond to the soothing, healing warmth.

Separateness disappears
as you enter into the experience of the fire.
You become intimately in tune with the fire.
And finally, you become one with the fire.
And it becomes one with you.

The chatter in your mind
and the tension in your body
are lulled away.
As you enter into
a state of luminous clarity and well-being
and your consciousness expands
to fill more reality
than you ordinarily experience.
Making love,
weeding your garden,
playing a musical instrument,
wandering along a deserted tropical beach,
and looking up unexpectedly on a starry night
and being overcome by the vastness and gloriousness,
are all meditations
if you fully enter into them.

Each can lift you
from yesterday's problems
and tomorrow's goal-directedness.

Each can undercut
your habitual image of yourself.

Each can change
your ordinary frame of reference
by centering you in the moment
that you are in.
And offer simple gates and pathways
into the all-expansive moment of now,
where you encounter
lower stress and higher awareness,
enlightenment, clarity, and peace.

Whenever one of these simple gates or pathways
almost accidentally
leads you into complete meditation,
the experience is so powerful and positive
that everyone usually wants more of it.
And through the years,
in response to the wanting,
a wide variety of meditation techniques
have been created
to capture at will
these rare spontaneous moments of bliss
and build them into
volitional patterns for everyday life.

There are meditations for active people.
Meditations for quiet people.
Meditations to enrich your body and your health.
Meditations to calm your emotions and stress.
Meditations to increase your mental power.
Meditations to develop your latent psychic heritage,
explore your dreams, and cross into past and future lives.
Meditations to bring you money and affluence.
Meditations to surround you with love, success,
serenity, and whatever else you desire.

You'll find these techniques
written as explorations
in this book,

so that you can read them
and try them from memory.
Or tape them
to play for yourself.
Or take turns
reading them and experiencing them
with a friend
or a small meditative group of friends.

Some of the meditative explorations
will work for you all of the time
and become standbys on a daily basis.
Most of them
will work for you some of the time
depending upon your degree of responsiveness
and the flexibility of your
personal belief systems.
But none of them
will work for you
unless you agree not to work too hard at them.
You see,
you can't work at meditation.
You just open up to the idea of it.
And allow any one of the techniques to carry you
into it.
Meditation
really isn't done
by doing anything.
It's done by being.
Especially by being
open to newness and change.

So if you try and try and try
and get mad at yourself
for doing it wrong or not getting it,
nothing will happen.
But if you can drift and flow into it
with an interested, expectant detachment
like a witness or an outside observer
instead of a student or a seeker,

you will quickly be overcome by it
and soon become very good at it.

To enter into complete meditation,
all you need to do is
set aside enough time to consider and try
each exploration that you respond to,
keep an open and receptive mind,
and begin to see how it feels
to believe that you can be.
Without having to do a single thing about it.

Other than that,
just expect the unexpected.
Complete meditation
will take you on a voyage of discovery
into many different moods,
uncharted attitudes and beliefs,
and unexplored layers
of consciousness and awareness.

As you begin to more fully experience
who you are,
where you are,
how you are feeling,
when you are tense and blocked,
and what you are asking for out of life,
you will develop more and more control.
Over your health.
Over your wants.
Over your creativity and self-expression.
And over your actual physical environment.

By practicing meditation
and being
completely who you are,
you will become more than you are now.
You will be
able to cross the next evolutionary bridge

and begin to develop the full potential
of your creaturehood.

It is the most exciting journey there is.
And this book will make it easier.
By helping you discover the inner avenues
that can take you
all the way you choose to go.
From wherever you are coming from.
To here. And now.

Beginning meditation

Beginning meditation

To meditate,
you need only two essentials
outside of yourself.
A place.
And a time.

Everything else in the outer world
is optional.

From time to time,
you may choose
an external object, person, or event
as a meditative subject.
But for now,
the right place and the right time
will start you on your way.

At this stage,
the right place will be any room
or portion of a room
that you set aside
especially for early meditative adventures.
In that place,
you might like to include
a chair or large floor pillow,
a soft rug,
and whatever else warms your spirit.
Like a flower, a candle,
a familiar or favorite possession,
or a picture.

Later on,
you won't need a special place.
Anywhere you are
becomes your special meditation place.
Whenever you choose to turn inward.

At this stage,
the right time will be any interval
that you specifically set aside
for meditation only.
Between fifteen minutes and a half hour
every morning and evening
before or long after meals
will be ideal.
You don't need to be rigid about it.
And you don't have to meditate
for the exact same number of minutes each time.

It does help a lot, however,
to be firm about setting the time aside
at approximately the same time of day
whether you choose to use it all
or not.
And to practice
one preliminary exploration from this chapter
with a meditation you know
once a day.
And a different preliminary exploration
with a new meditation you haven't tried before,
one other time each day.

In other words,
don't grind away at the same thing
day after day after day.
The fun and the exhilaration
you get from meditating
comes from being flexible
and constantly open to a variety of experiences.

Later on,
you won't need a special time.
Any time at all
becomes your special meditation time.
Whenever you choose to turn inward.

Other than place and time,
everything else you need to meditate
you already have.
Inside.
And in this chapter,
you'll find all the preliminaries
and warm-up exercises
you need
to activate
your own inner resources.
And begin meditation.

Meditation positions

Any position
that keeps the right and left side
of your body in equal balance
and that you can maintain comfortably
without moving
for the length of your meditation
is the right position for you.
Of course,
even an uncomfortable position
can become a creative experience
by allowing you to meditate
on your state of discomfort.
So once again,
there are no rules.
Instead, there is one basic principle.

You are constantly
taking energy in from your universe,
storing it,
and discharging it
back into the universe again.
Converting energy into life and matter
and life and matter into energy
is every physical creature's fundamental role.

When you meditate,
the energy exchange is amplified
and greatly heightened.
Which explains why
complete meditation
is so truly enlightening and invigorating.

To smooth out the energy amplification
and make it easier on yourself,
your meditation position
must ultimately allow you to lose
whatever sense of separation or alienation
you experience in your universe.
That's why you keep both sides of your body
in balance.
By not crossing one leg over the other.
And not folding your arms protectively
in front of you.
That's also why
as you harmonize yourself within your space
through your position and your breath,
you expand your personal energy
and your inner power base
to remarkable degrees.

Experiment
with the meditation positions that follow
to find the ones
that help you to flow into expansiveness
with a minimum of resistance.

Sitting

A favorite traditional position
for meditation
is sitting.
In a straightbacked chair.
Or on the floor.

In a chair,
sit erect and straighten your spine.
Place both feet squarely on the floor
a comfortable distance apart.
If you're not wearing shoes,
so much the better.
Loosen your collar, your belt,
and anything else
that prevents you from breathing
freely, easily, and deeply
into your diaphragm and abdomen.
Allow both hands to fall loosely
in your lap.

Tilt your head back a little
so that your neck and spine form
one continuous vertical line.
Then close your eyes gently
And look up at the inside of your forehead.

For now,
just experience how it feels
to sit like this.
Notice where you are touching the chair
and where you are not.
Sense the floor under your feet
and the solid support it offers.
Connect with the sensual caress of the air
on your skin.
Experience it. And that's all.

On the floor
or on a floor pillow,
sit erect and straighten your spine.
Cross your legs Indian style.
And let your hands rest loosely in your lap,
like empty gloves.
Tilt your head back a little.
Close your eyes and look up
at the inside of your forehead.

If you like,
try the half lotus position
by resting one foot
on top of the other thigh
or in the cleft of the other bent leg.
The full lotus
with both legs intertwined
is for expert yogis only.
It's uncomfortable and completley unnecessary
for complete meditation.

For now,
just experience how it feels to sit like this.
Notice the cushion or floor under you.
And the air flowing around and through you.
That's all.

Squatting

Stand
with your heels about a foot apart.
Your feet may be straight
or pointed in or out at 45° angles,
whichever is more comfortable.
Keep your heels flat on the floor.
Exhale your breath
and slowly bend your knees,
sinking down toward the floor
until your knees are completley bent
and resting under the sockets of your armpits.
Join your hands loosely
or let them hang freely in front of you.

Tip your head back a little.
Close your eyes
and look up inside your forehead.
Notice how easily you can breathe
deeply into your diaphragm.

Squatting becomes easier
and more natural to you
as you practice it.
It's worth learning
because it brings
your positive and negative polarities
into balance.
Making you a more effective energy vessel
and a better storage battery.

For now,
just experience these sensations
for a moment or two.

Standing

For centuries,
the star pose
has been a primary posture for energy exchange.
And for recharging and rejuvenating the body.
In his sketches,
Leonardo Da Vinci immortalized it.
In your meditation place,
it can immortalize you
by helping you maintain a radiant inner glow
and an easy access to complete meditation.

Stand
with your spine straight,
your pelvis aligned under you,
your feet further apart than your shoulders
or as far apart as you can place them
without locking your knees.

Tip your head slightly back.
Keep your eyes open for balance,
but allow your gaze to unfocus.
Raise your arms,

keeping them straight,
until your elbows are above your shoulders
and your hands
are in line with the top of your head.

Turn your left palm down
and your right palm up.

Breathe deeply into your diaphragm.
And experience yourself filling to capacity,
then overflowing
with newfound energy.

Lying down

Let your legs
spread slightly apart
with your toes and feet hanging loosely
from your ankles.
Let your hands fall to your sides,
palms up.
Sense how straight your spine is.
Notice what parts of you are in contact
with the floor
and what parts you are holding up,
like the small of your back, your neck
and maybe the back of your knees.
But don't do anything about it.
Just lie there
and feel the air moving
over and around and throughout your body.
As you breathe deeply and quietly
into your diaphragm.

Tubbing

Run the water in your bathtub
as hot as you can stand it
until it's nearly full.
Or get in
and let the hot water fill up
all around you.

Lie back.
With your knees spread apart,
resting against the sides of the tub,
and your ankles crossed loosely
near the faucet.
Let the sloping end of the tub
support your head.
Let your hands and arms float.
Let your body float up and sink slowly down again
as you breathe evenly and deeply
into your diaphragm and abdomen.

Float and drift with your eyes closed.
Submerge your ears
and listen to the throbbing beat of your heart.
Sense how the heat of the water
relaxes your body, calms your thoughts,
and raises your inner vibrational level.
You will use these heightened vibrations later.
Just become aware of them
for now.

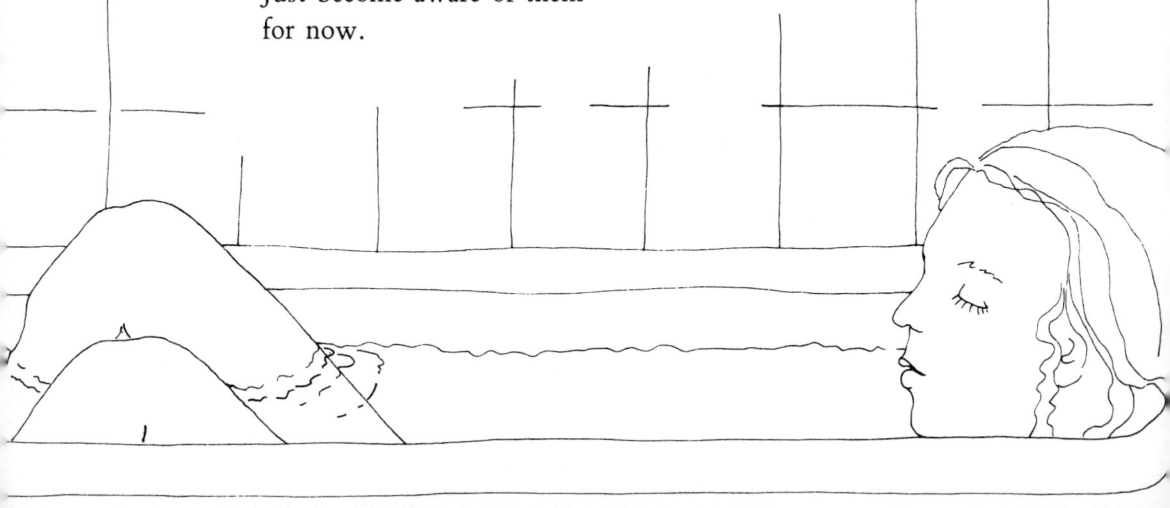

Alignment

Whenever you are in alignment
with the magnetic axis
of the earth,
you will find yourself flowing more freely
into a fundamental unity
with the space around you.

Getting aligned is easy.
Always meditate facing north
when you are standing or sitting.
When you are lying flat,
let the top of your head point north,
like the needle of the compass you use
to check your directions.

Magnetic alignment
is the path of least resistance
to meditating.
And to interphasing your life energy
with the energies all around you.

Breathing

Sometime after birth
but before conscious memory,
you forgot how to breathe.
You stopped breathing
slowly, rhythmically, deeply,
way down low in your diaphragm
like babies, puppies,
and most other living creatures do.
And you started breathing
shallow and fast
way up in your upper chest,
unable to fully satisfy
your body's primal need for oxygen.

Shallow breathing chokes off
spiritual development
and evolutionry growth.
And makes complete meditation
impossible.

The three breathing explorations that follow
will reopen your channels
of intuition and spontaneity,
allow you to live more fully
and more fully energized,
and simplify the meditative process
enormously.

Try each of them at least once
with each meditation position.
Then use whichever one comes most easily
for a while.
When you find yourself experiencing
a meditation block,
change to another breathing mode.
And the block will open for you.
Changing your breath pattern
always shifts your state of consciousness
and amplifies your awareness
beyond any problem area.

Basic breathing

Place your hands just under your ribs
with your fingertips touching.
Bend over from your waist.

Inhale through your nose.
And send all the air to your fingertips.
Feel them separate as your diaphragm expands.
Then feel your ribs separate.
And sense your chest expanding.
Hold your breath for a moment.

Then release your breath.
As you exhale through your nose,
feel your fingertips come together
as your diaphragm flattens.
Sense your ribs coming together
and feel your chest lower.

Repeat this same breathing sequence
until it becomes natural and effortless.
And then
try it in each meditation position.
Sense how each of the positions
amplifies and strengthens
each basic breath you take.
As you practice,
begin to place a stronger and stronger emphasis
on exhalation.

First inhale to a silent count of four.
Hold for a silent count of four
before you exhale.
Exhale to a silent count of eight.

Inhale again to a silent count of four.
Hold for a count of four.
But exhale to a silent count of eight.
Experience your breath.
Think only of your breath.
And the rhythmic cycle of your breathing.

Increase the silent exhalation count
to sixteen
on your next breath,
experiencing the long and steady
outgoing flow of your energy.
Experiment.
Four counts in.
Four counts holding.
And between 16 and 32 counts
for each exhalation.

The right number of counts for you
is the number that releases
your inner resistance and relaxes
and revitalizes you.

Make that count
your count.
Exlore it fully.
And become increasingly aware of how you feel
as you sense your breath
beginning to clear your mind.

Foundation breathing

Like the four sides of a pyramid base,
there are four sides to foundation breathing.

Inhale through your nose
and allow the air to flow
directly and completely
to your diaphragm.
Just as before.
But time your breath to a silent count
of seven.
Hold for a count of seven.

Then place your tongue
lightly against the roof of your mouth.
And exhale through your mouth
to a silent count of seven.
Notice the gentle hissing sound
as your breath flows around your tongue.
Explore the aftermath of the sound
for another silent count
of seven,
before you inhale again.

Maintain a steady four-part cycle.
Seven counts in.
Seven counts holding in.
Seven counts out.
Seven counts holding out.
After you establish the rhythm,
try foundation breathing
in each meditation position.

Often
as few as ten complete foundation breathing cycles
are enough
to lull you into a meditative state.
If that happens,
just enjoy it.
If that doesn't happen yet,
Just enjoy the fact that
it will happen soon enough.

Breathing is the beginning
of being in meditation.
You are well on your way.

Reverse breathing

Basic breathing and foundation breathing
are essentially
relaxation cycles of breath.
They soothe and release
the tensions of body and soul.
They allow meditation
to flow over you
like a warm waveless tide.

After you are able to
drift into each of their rhythms
simply and naturally,
you may want to explore

a more active, more controlled
cycle of meditative breathing.
Reverse breathing.

Place your hands just under your ribs
with your fingertips touching.
Bend over from your waist.

Pull in your abdomen as tight as you can
so your fingertips overlap.
Hold it in
as you inhale through your nose.
Feel your ribs separate
and your chest expand.
Feel the resistance
as your breath pushes against
your tightened abdomen.
Hold your abdomen in
and hold your breath.

Then exhale through your mouth
with the tip of your tongue against the roof of your mouth.
And at the same time,
push your abdomen out as far as you can.
Feel your fingertips separate
as your ribs come together
and your chest lowers.

Repeat the reverse breathing cycle
a few times
until you can do it
without thinking too much about it.

Then combine it with
each meditation position
and begin to time it out.

Inhale to a silent count of four.
Hold for a silent count of four.
Exhale for a silent count of eight.

Continue to inhale for four counts
and to hold for four counts.
But gradually
increase your exhalation count
to a comfortable place between 16 and 32.

Reverse breathing doesn't
make much sense
until you really get into it.
Then you discover
that by pushing the energy
of each breath that you inhale
up
into your chest and neck and head,
you ignite a fuse
that will blast meditative blocks
forever out of sight and out of mind.

Relaxation

Each area of tension in your body
is an area where energy
is trapped and blocked from flowing
freely and creatively within you.

Meditation will ultimately
enable you to take your tensions
one by one
and release them.
Knowing this,
your tensions
will attempt to inhibit your meditation
for all they are worth.

So,
in the beginning,
you need to calm your tensions
to the point where they
and you

allow yourself to relax
into complete meditation.

If you don't know how it feels to be
completely relaxed,
a Complete Relaxation exploration
is reprinted in the appendix,
along with a special technique
that can reactivate the feeling anytime.
And anyplace.
Try it now.

You will never go wrong
if you devote
the first five to ten minutes
of every meditation
to relaxation.
By quietly allowing your breath
and your awareness
to flow zone by zone by zone
from your toes
up to your head.

You can combine your relaxation
with the counts of your breathing cycle
in any meditation position.
Like this.

Inhale and send your breath to your feet.
Hold.
Exhale and allow your feet to relax.
Forget about your feet.

Inhale and send your breath
spiraling through your legs, knees, and thighs.
Hold.
Exhale and allow them to relax.
Forget about your legs, knees, and thighs.
Inhale and send your breath
to your hips, genitals, and abdomen.

Hold.
Exhale and allow them to relax.
Forget about your hips, genitals, and abdomen.

Inhale and send your breath
billowing through your stomach and chest.
Hold.
Exhale and allow them to relax.
Forget about your stomach and chest.

Inhale and send your breath up your spine.
Hold.
Exhale and allow your spine to relax.
Forget about your spine.

Inhale and send your breath
through your shoulders, elbows, and forearms.
Hold.
Exhale and allow them to relax.
Forget about your shoulders, elbows,
and forearms.

Inhale and send your breath
through your wrists and hands
and out your fingertips.
Hold.
Exhale and allow your wrists and hands
to relax.
Forget about your wrists and hands.

Inhale and send your breath to your neck.
Hold.
Exhale and allow your neck to relax.
Forget about your neck.
From the neck down
you can now hardly feel anything
but heavier and heavier and heavier.

Inhale and send your breath
drifting behind the mask that is your face.
Hold.
Exhale and allow your face to relax.
Forget about your face.

Inhale and send your breath all through your head.
Hold.
Exhale and allow your head to relax.
Forget about your head.

Now you are completely relaxed.
And now you can go on.

Alpha

By relaxing in your meditation position
and fortifying and empowering the process
with meditative breathing,
you may unexpectedly find yourself
in alpha,
where all but physically active mediation,
involving a shift
from the left side of your brain to
the right side,
occurs.

Alpha
is the state in which
your brain produces alpha waves.
They measure and cycle
slower and deeper than the beta waves
of everyday waking activity,
yet faster than the theta waves of sleep
and delta waves of unconsciousness.
So alpha is the narrow but infinite plane
between being awake and being asleep.
It is here that you will derive

the most pleasure
and the most spectacular results
from meditation.
For all practical purposes,
being in alpha is
being in complete meditation.

And one final preliminary warm-up
will get you all the way into it.

Clearing

Just as relaxation
calms your body interference
to allow free-flowing, fully energized meditation,
clearing
calms your intellectual interference
and mental chatter.

Meditation involves being.
Complete meditation involves being completely
in the moment that you are actually in.
Specifically, the now moment of your life.

Now
is always where you are.
But frequently,
your mind is before now,
stuck on rerunning a tape
of some recent emotionally-charged experience.
Just as frequently,
your mind is ahead of now,
stuck in creating a worry or problem
of some possible future moment yet to come
that may or may not
actually involve you when you get there.

Clearing
will do exactly what it says.
You create a visual screen
on the inside of your forehead
for your meditational field of view.
And you proceed to clear it.
And to keep it clear.
On a day by day basis.

Like this.

Clearing yesterday

Choose a meditation position
and breathing pattern.
And stick with them through this exploration.
Relax your body zone by zone.

Then,
on the space on the inside of your forehead,
the space your closed eyes are looking up at,
visualize an empty screen.

On that screen,
begin to see yourself as you were
when you woke up yesterday
if you are meditating in the morning.
Or as you were this morning
if it is now night.
Starting with the opening of your eyes,
visualize as many events of the day
as you can.
Hour by hour.
See as clearly as you can remember
what you wore,
what you ate for breakfast,
how the day passed.

Rerun the whole tape of the whole day.
Moments of joy and warmth.
Moments of panic and embarrassment.
Moments of gray nothing.

Watch your rerun impartially.
With no explanation.
No rationalizations.
No labels.
No self criticism.
No judgements about your behavior.
Simply become a witness
of your daily tape
without trying to understand or analyze it,
as if you're watching a rerun
of some vaguely familiar television show.

When you have run your tape completely,
you will be up to where you are
right now.
So let go of your tape at that point.
That's all.

The events of the day will leave you.
Free of guilt.
Free of remorse.
Free.
To go on in the moment you are in
now.
And complete meditation.

Clearing tomorrow

A simple variation will help
if you are stuck on a future event
and cannot release it from your mind.

Follow the same steps.
A position.
A breathing pattern.
A zone by zone relaxation.

Then look at your screen.
And cue up your tape
about tomorrow's events.

Start when you wake up.
Notice how you will get out of bed.
What you wear.
What you eat.
See yourself living through the day to come,
right up to the event you are stuck on.

See the moment of that event coming up on your tape.
And watch how you choose to handle it.

Keep your tape running past the event.
And finish out the day.
Watch what you decide to do that evening.
See yourself go to bed.
Fall asleep.
Then turn off tomorrow's tape.
And let it go.

Whatever comes,
you'll deal with it
one way or another.
For now,
get back to now.
And complete meditation.

Clearing now

If you would like to experience
this one moment of your life
more clearly than ever before,

and use it as a diving board into meditation,
begin here.
And begin now.

Choose your position
and breathing pattern.
Relax your body zone by zone.
Then give your breath permission
to continue the pattern
on its own.
Automatically.

Open your eyes
and in a non-selective way
begin to see whatever is before you.
Explore your entire field of vision.

Hold your vision in full focus.
Begin to listen.
Allow each sound you hear
to link up with its appropriate object
if you can see it without moving.
If you can't see it,
place each sound with its source
in your mind.
But maintain the complete focus
of your eyes and ears.

Still holding your awareness
at its present level,
blend in all the other sensations around you.
Notice the pressure of your clothing
on your body.
Notice where your body feels warm,
where it feels cool,
where it feels no feeling at all.
Notice any odors in the air.
Notice the taste of the roof of your mouth
and the insides of your cheeks.

Notice everything that fills this moment
and makes it so brilliantly alive.

Allow all of your perceptions
to integrate with each other.
Bring them all together,
like a conductor calls forth
all the varied sounds
of a symphony orchestra.
If one sensation captures your attention,
let it go.
And try to bring a less noticeable one
into full focus.
Hold it all.
And allow it all to build and build
until it forms
an indescribably bright moment of clarity.

Then,
suddenly,
close your eyes
and let it all go.

Follow any one sensation if you like.
The ticking of a clock.
The cool air on your forehead.
And allow it to take you where it will.
Lose yourself and drift in it.

Then,
just as suddenly,
open your eyes.
And snap back
into fully integrated focus.
Taking in all the perceivable sensations
all around you.
All at once.

Shift back and forth
as many times as you like.
Conclude the exploration out of focus
if you want to go deeper
into meditation.
Or in full focus
if you want to stop meditating.

Either way,
you will be clear.
And you will be clearly centered
right now
in your own beingness.
And in complete harmony
with the principles of
complete meditation.

All together now

At first,
each preliminary warm-up element
may take up an entire meditation period.

Trust the process.

With practice,
the five elements
of position, alignment, breathing, relaxing and clearing
will flow together
almost automatically overlapping each other.
And lowering you gently into alpha
in less than ten minutes.

You'll take your position,
knowing you are aligned to the north.
You'll settle into your breathing pattern,
simultaneously relaxing your body
in just a few breaths.

You'll clear your mind
of a day that passed if you're stuck there
or a day to come if you're stuck there.
Or you'll clear the moment you are in
so that you can stick there as long as you like.
Now.
And you'll be ready
for each big new meditational adventure
of each new day.

Coming out of meditation will be
even easier.
You'll simply
let your inner screen go dim
or draw a curtain across it,
open your eyes very gently,
and allow the moment you are in
to form in full focus and full clarity
all around you.

The meditative exlorations that follow
assume that your preliminaries
are all working for you.
Take the time
now
to be sure they are before you go on.

Easy meditation

Easy meditation

All of the preliminaries and warm-ups
you've just explored in the last section
will ultimately allow you to enter
voluntarily complete meditation
whenever you wish.
They are gates
into many of the advanced meditation
explorations
yet to come.

Some meditations
however,
including some of the meditations in this section,
are so easy
that you can just
involuntarily
drift off into them.

Easy meditations
are like anything easy.
They're fun.
They're relaxing.
And they're good for you
in the sense that
anything easy and pleasurable
is its own reward.

As you'll soon see.

Affirmations in alpha

At least twice a day,
every living creature
enters a state of
complete meditation.

Automatically.
Including you.

It happens
right on that fine fine line
between being awake
and being asleep.
On that line,
your brain slips into
an alpha wave cycle
on its way from beta to theta at night.
Or theta to beta in the morning.

You are most apt to notice
your easy alpha state
in the morning.
You're on the sleep-to-waking line
and you turn off your alarm
and roll over thinking to yourself,
"If I go back to sleep,
I'll miss my train
and be late for work."

Late and embarrassed,
two hours later
you've experienced the power
of complete meditation.
Which is:
the thoughts that you implant
in alpha
always materialize in reality.

If you play
with these two-a-day
easy meditative states,
you'll learn to lengthen
the line between
sleeping and waking.

And you'll begin to experience
some of the positive benefits
of meditation
in your life.

For instance.

Every night
as you drift into sleep,
visualize an alarm clock
on the screen
on the back of your forehead.
See your hands
setting the alarm on the clock,
to the time you want to wake up.
And say to yourself:
I will wake up at six-fifteen,
or whatever time you choose,
tomorrow morning
feeling alive and refreshed.

When you wake up,
it will be six-fifteen
or whatever time you chose.
And you will feel
more alive and refreshed
than ever before.

As you set your clock,
the variations are endless.
You may get as specific as:
I will wake up at six-fifteen
tomorrow morning
and the calcium deposit
behind my left knee cap
will vaporize in the light of day.
And if you catch the edge of alpha
right on the line,

your calcium deposit will shrink
each day
until it's gone.

In the morning,
as you pass through alpha,
be conscious of what you leave there.
One positive affirmation a day
will begin to produce
incredible changes in your life.
You might say to yourself:
today I will find someone to love
who will love me back.
Or:
Today I will feel better
than I have ever felt before.
Or:
Today unexpected money
will come into my life.

One affirmation each morning.
One other affirmation each night
as you set your inner clock.
And in no time
you will begin to have
the things you want
showing up all around you.
As if by magic.

Concentration

Intense, highly focused concentration
on a single point or single object
gives you easy access
to complete meditation.

One object at a time

Take any object you enjoy looking at.
Perhaps a flower,
a ring, a symbol, a sculpture,
or a design.
Set it in front of you
as you sit in a chair with your back straight.
Or in a comfortable cross-legged position.

Focus your eyes
on your object.
And keep them there,
blinking whenever you have to.
Think
only of the object you are looking at.

Notice
its color,
its shape,
its function,
the way its lines flow and blend,
its highlights and shadows.
Other thoughts will attempt
to interfere.
Send them away gently.
Just let them flow off your movie screen.

Tell your thoughts,
"I am busy now
and have no time for you.
Please come back later."
And let your mind return to your object.

Stay with it for a whole minute
at first.
Gradually,
let yourself stay with it
up to three minutes or more.

The candle flame

Sit.
On the floor
in a comfortable cross-legged position.
Or in a chair.
Place a lighted candle
two to four feet in front of you.
Fix your gaze upon the flame
as you breathe your basic relaxation breath.

Observe
how the flame flickers and dances
and moves with wondrous subtlety.

Notice the colors of the flame.
Blue on the bottom.
Dark orange at the center.
Glowing red at the wick.
Then gold
and lighter orange.

Notice
the aura of the flame,
how it spreads
and touches you with its glow.

Keep watching the flame
for about two minutes
as you breathe your basic relaxation breath.
And send all other thoughts
gently away.

Then
close your eyes.
And place your palms
lightly over your lids.
After a moment,

the afterimage of the flame
will form in the blackness as you watch.

Catch it.
And try to center it
evenly on your movie screen
on the inside of your forehead
just above your eyes.

Don't force the image.
Just let it shimmer and glow
and be.

Observe
how your flame
flickers and dances
and moves with wondrous subtlety.

If your flame disappears,
you can will it to come back to your screen.
And it will come back to your screen.

Notice the colors of your flame.
Blue on the bottom.
Dark orange at the center.
Glowing red at the wick.
Then gold
and lighter orange.

Notice the aura of your flame.

Hold the image for about two minutes.
When you let it begin to fade,
notice
the tiny changes in its form and color.

Lower your hands.
Open your eyes ever so slowly.
Sense how refreshed you feel.

Become aware
of what it's like
for your mind to be alert and relaxed,
both at the same time.

Silent mantras

Concentration on a silent repetitive sound or mantra
in your head
is another gate to complete meditation,
popularized under the name Transcendental Meditation™.

Try it now,
and sense the magic working in your mind.

To begin,
sit
with your spine erect
in a comfortable chair.

Uncross your legs
and place both feet on the floor.
Place your hands in your lap,
with your fingers unclasped.
Loose and relaxed.

See yourself completely relaxed.
Feel yourself completely relaxed
from your head
all the way down to your toes.

Let wave after wave of relaxation
wash over you
each time you exhale.
Let the waves carry
all your tension, pressure, fear, and worry
away.
Concentrate only on your breathing
as you breathe your basic relaxation breath
slowly and deeply,
slowly and deeply.

Let your breathing deepen even more.
And begin to say to yourself
your silent mantra
in rhythm
to each inhalation
and each exhalation.

You could try this mantra:
Hum. . . So. . .
It means
I am the one.
Say HUM
with every inhalation.
And say SO
with every exhalation.

Or you could try this mantra:
One. . . Two. . .
ONE as you inhale.
TWO as you exhale.

Or you could try
any peaceful or beautiful thought.
Like:
I AM (inhale)
LOVED (exhale)

Or:
I AM (inhale)
FILLED WITH LIGHT (exhale).

Or:
RE- (Inhale)
LAX (exhale)

Just sit.
Just be.
And breathe your basic relaxation breath,
repeating your silent mantra
over and over,
and over and over,
and over and over.

If any thoughts intrude,
send them gently away
or let them drift off your movie screen,
leaving it blank.
Say to yourself, "Oh well . . . "
And return to your mantra.

This exploration,
twice a day,
for ten to twenty minutes each time,
will help you
gain and keep control
of your mind's on/off switch.

And allow your mind
to let the rest of you
be.

Sound mantras

Sounds
and the vibrations
that center sounds produce
can relax your mind
and keep you feeling clear
and refreshed.
When tension resounds all around you,
mantras like these
can create soothing vibrations
and harmonious calm within you.

Try sound mantras softly
or loud.
But try them.

Om.
You pronounce it long and slowly
as you exhale:

AH—OH—MMMMMMMMMM

Start it deep inside
with a low low note of a musical scale.

Then try higher notes.
As you sit with your spine erect,
sense which parts of your body
vibrate in tune with which notes.
Om is the universal sound.
It means everything there is.

Shanti.
You pronounce it
with both syllables accented evenly:

SHAWN—TEA.

Chant it slowly
like a little song
that you could have skipped roped to
very slowly,
as a child.

Keep the SHAN
always on the same musical note
and let the TI
fall two notes below it
or rise one note above it.

There is no right or wrong way.
Your ear will tell you what to do.

Shanti
means peace.
And it brings peace and harmony
into your life.
Chanted slowly,
you can sense the peaceful vibrations
flowing like ripples on clear water
from your innermost self
beyond the surface of your body.
Surrounding you with a sea of calm
relaxation.

Go binda.
You pronounce it just the way it looks.
And say it in a fast chant
in cycles of seven times
like this,
letting your whole mouth
move with the syllables:

GO BIN-DA, GO BIN-DA, GO BIN-DA,
GO BIN-DA,
GO BIN-DA, GO BIN-DA,
GO BIN-DA. (And the DA is very loud.)

If you say the chant over and over
for ten to twenty minutes,
with your spine straight,
the backs of your hands touching
in front of you
and your thumbs pointed down,
you can release all the tension
in your face as well as your mind.
And you can keep depression and negativity
far from your mind and body.

Go binda means,
mental unrest and depression,
let me be.
It is the eastern equivalent of:
Blues stay away from my door.
And it will help you to remain
happy, healthy,
and whole.

Music

Sit
in a comfortable chair
and close your eyes.

Listen
to a recorded piece of music
for five minutes
as you breathe your basic relaxation breath.
Immerse yourself in the music.
Listen so carefully

and so completely
that you lose all outside thoughts.

If visualizations of the music
form in your head,
send them gently away.

Just listen
and become one with the sound,
like an instrument
through which the music flows.
Tell yourself
it's all right not to hear or understand
or analyze
either the music or the experience.

Just listen.
As you let the sound
encompass you.

Afterwards,
become aware of the great and tiny wonders
of which you can partake.
By the earful.

Symbols

Simple visual symbols
that date back to antiquity
and ahead to eons yet to come
are still other easy gates
into complete meditation.
Their power lies in their universality
as archetypes.
And as you sit
in a comfortable meditation position
and focus completely

on each one
for two to five minutes,
you will find
that you can directly experience
what an archetype is
without needing to understand it.

Symbols:

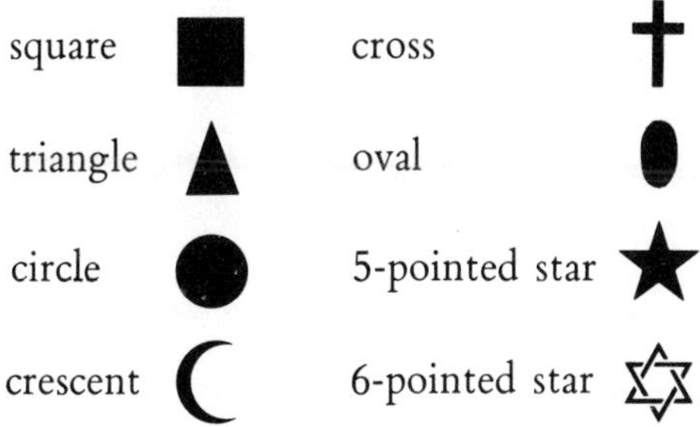

Fantasy visualizations

Another timeless way to drift
into easy meditation
is by creating fantasy visualizations
on your inner screen.
And then projecting them outward
to fill the space around you.
In many primitive cultures,
this is considered an advanced art.
In our own culture,
it is called daydreaming
and discouraged as
a sure sign of laziness.

Fantasy visualization
can take you to any place
on earth
or beyond.
It can easily immerse you
in complete meditation.

Shift into the meditation position
that is most comfortable for you.
And see for yourself.
In the five explorations that follow.

The beach

With your eyes closed,
notice the screen
on the inside of your forehead.
Allow your screen to go blank.

Extend your screen down to your feet.
And notice the sand you are standing on.
Take in its color and texture.
Extend your gaze to the left.
Follow the contour of the sand
and the land down to the water's edge
for as far as the inner eye can see.
Notice any trees, driftwood, dunes
or dunegrass.
Be aware of where the beach disappears
around a bend into the ocean
or on the horizon.

Extend your gaze in front of you.
And fill in the ocean.
Notice whether the water is turbulent
or smooth with small rippling waves.
Observe how the color of the water changes
as you look outward
to the horizon line.

Look up at the sky.
Notice the color
and the cloud formations.
See where the sun is
and begin to feel its warmth.
Feel also the breeze from the water.

Fill in all the details.
The birds, other living beings.
And then, create a blanket at your feet.
Lie down on it.
And enjoy your beach for as long as you like.

The woods

On your inner screen,
form a portion of a forest.
Allow your screen to expand
as if you were watching a scene
on television
where the camera zooms back suddenly.
And begin to notice
all the varieties and thicknesses
of all the trees
all around you.

Notice also
where the patches of sunlight or moonlight
appear through the denseness.

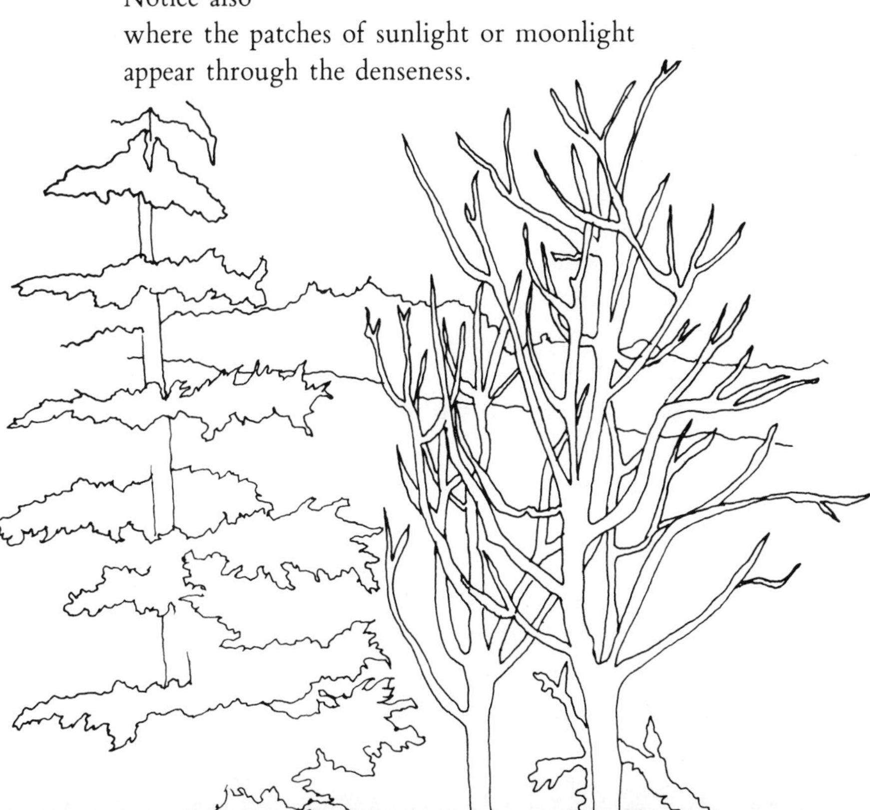

Feel the stones, the moss, the cool moist earth
beneath your feet.
Look up
over your head
to the soft green leafy cover
with occasional flecks of sky beyond.
Observe the sounds and scents of life
all around you.
Reach out and touch the rough bark
of a nearby tree
and sense how time must feel
to a tree.

Walk through your woods,
experiencing and savoring
the sensations of eternal life and growth.

The brook

Observe on your inner screen,
a brook.
Watch it flowing
cold and clear and quickly
over stones and submerged logs,
through larger rock formations,
around boulders.
Follow the brook.
Across a meadow,
green with new spring grass,
alive with flowers,
and, perhaps, speckled with cows.

Experience the life within the brook
and all along its banks.

Allow your consciousness
to merge with the consciousness
of the brook

as it meanders across the landscape
on its journey
from its source to its destination.

The desert

Imagine on your inner screen
an endless expanse of granite
disintegrating to sand.

Extend your screen in all directions
until you can feel it
under your feet
and see it
no matter which way you look.

Let huge piles of rocks appear
here and there
like crumbling primordial statues.
And acres and acres of sagebrush
and tumbleweed,
spread out endlessly
against muted shades of brown and orange.

Begin to fill in the details.
Observe the more subtle colors appear
as sharp, clean, clearly differentiated
flashes
of shimmering beauty.
Sense the slow undulating rhythym
like the tides of an ancient dustfilled sea.
And the vastness of the sky.

In legend,
each man was required
to pass through the desert
in order to emerge
with fully flowering consciousness.

You can begin to do just that.
Right now.

The city

Allow the screen
inside your forehead
to take on the appearance of
an empty window.
And look through it
into the city.
Not the city you live in now.
But the city of your imagination.

You might form your city
from any dimly remembered or still-to-come
period of history.
Or from any place in the world
or in the galaxy
right now.

Observe the buildings.
Then move through the open window
of your screen
into the streets below.
Walk through
or glide above this city of your creation.

Notice the people and their clothing,
the transportation they use.
Let the details form,
cementing the image,
and enjoy each of the varied sensations
your city has to offer.

The paradox of environment

Now that you know
that you can quite literally create
any environment you choose,
whenever you want,
as you've just seen and done,
your physical location for meditating
will become less and less important
as you go on
from here.
Anywhere you are
is the perfect place for you to be.
And a place environmentally suited to
complete meditation.

Religious meditation

Religious meditation

Whether its a mountain top
or a cathedral,
the experience of being
in your place of worship,
when you enter into it completely and openly,
is the same
as the experience of complete meditation.

And many people
who feel blocked, frustrated, or turned off
by the idea of meditation
do it regularly
when and where they pray.

The only difference is:
In meditation
you allow yourself to become one
with the object of your meditation
or with the all that is
in the universe.
And in religious prayer,
you allow yourself to become one
with your god.
So the only difference is
that there is no difference.

Meditation is not a substitute
for religious feeling.
It is an amplification technique.
You will discover that
it enables you to stay on
your path
and strengthen it.

As you can see for yourself
in this section,

the varieties of religious experience
are as endless as
the varieties of complete meditation.

Your place of worship

Wherever you go to pray is
your place of worship.
And God is there for you whether you're in
a medieval European cathedral,
a stark New England church,
a synagogue, a mosque, an oriental temple,
a colorful Saint's Day street festival,
an outdoor firelit circle,
a 200-foot stone pyramid
or a cave.

When you are in a place that is
specifically consecrated or set aside
for worship,
the energy of your environment
serves to focus you
single-pointedly
on your objective.
And everything in the atmosphere
can ease you into your religious experience.

Notice for yourself
next time you are in your place of worship
how the music and artifacts and decor,
the incense or imagined fragrance in the air,
the sound of the words of the service,
and the patterns or pictures in your mind,
all serve to open you up to
an encounter with your god.

The rosary

Sit quietly as Catholics do, with a string of rosary beads.
Tune in to the presence of the beads
in your hands,
with your eyes closed.

As you pass the string of beads slowly
through your fingers,
notice how the smaller beads
are periodicaly punctuated by
larger beads.
Each time your fingers
come to rest on a small bead,
softly say:
Hail Mary, full of grace,
The Lord is with thee.
Blessed art thou among women
And blessed is the fruit of thy womb, Jesus.
Hail Mary, Mother of God,
Pray for us sinners now
And at the hour of our death.
Amen.

Move on to another small bead
and repeat the words of the prayer.
And when your fingers touch a large bead,
say instead:
Our Father who art in heaven,
Hallowed be thy name.
Thy kingdom come, thy will be done
On earth as it is in heaven.
Give us this day our daily bread
And forgive us our trespasses
As we forgive those who trespass against us.
Lead us not into temptation
And deliver us from evil.
For Thine is the kingdom and the power
And the glory
Forever.

Move on to a smaller bead,
repeating the first prayer.
And continue around the beads
for 20 minutes.
Notice the meditative effects.
And the meditative effectiveness.

Davening

From deep in the mysticism
of orthodox Judiasm,
ritual morning chants still fill the air
proclaiming the almightiness
of the Almighty.
And the oneness of God and All That Is.

The power of davening
is in the lilting musical vibrations
that bring you closer to God
and carry the words that mean:
Our Father, Our King, we have no other.
Imagine yourself
facing the east,
visualizing the great wall of Jerusalem,
swaying and moving your body with each breath,
and repeating for 15 to 20 minutes
in a wailing, primal, musical tone
these words:
Al-vay-nu Mal-kay-nu
Ain La-nu Mel-lech
Ain La-nu Mel-lech
A-la Ah-tah

Eastern affirmation

More than 200 million Buddhists
reaffirm their connection with the universe
each day,

seated before small altars.
They repeat words like these
over and over
with a droning hive-like rhythm and tone
for two to six hours at a time.
Which totally clears their minds for
communications from God.
Try it now for as long as you like:

Nam yo ho ren-gay keyo.

The eyes of god

In Egypt more than 20 centuries ago,
energized by prayer within the great pyramid,
the high priest would appear
with the great ankh in his hand
and the countenance of god in his eyes.
You can recreate the effect
on your inner screen
or by looking into the eyes of the face
of your favorite religious portrait.

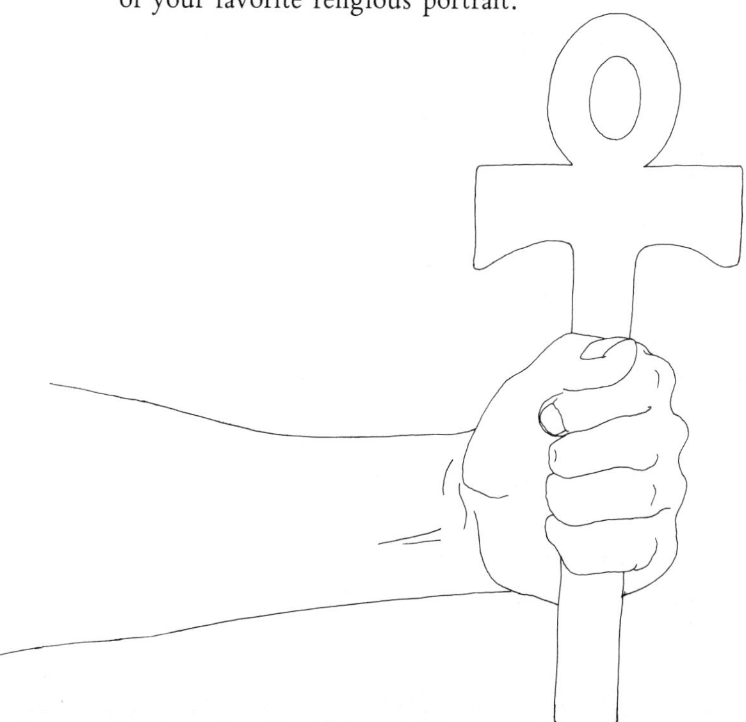

See the eyes before you now.
Deep blue,
with overtones of midnight
shifting to black.
Bottomless.
Like the eyes that encompass
all the stars in the endless sky
of a clear summer night.

The eyes are endlessly deep and penetrating.
With nothing individualized or personal
in them.
And yet, you are in them.
Along with the world and all creation.
And as you are in these eyes,
these eyes and the countenance behind them
are in your eyes.
The watcher and the watched
are in complete unity and harmony,
sharing an infinite field
of unquestionable love.

A ritual of nature

When Indians freely walked
the lands of North America,
there was an essential purity of contact
between man and nature
and between men and gods.

Young Indians approaching maturity
participated in a deep and silent meditation
that lasted two days and two nights.
You won't need to explore this ritual of nature
out in the world
to share the benefits of it,
if you visualize yourself
exploring it now
on your inner screen.

Just before sunrise,
seek out the highest summit
in your area.
Stand there.
Naked, erect, silent, and motionless,
facing the East,
awaiting the first rays of the sun
as they sparkle and dance over the horizon.

Stand there and watch.
Without moving.
As the sun travels up over your head
and down behind you.

Remain there through the night.
Standing naked, erect, silent, and motionless.
And through the next day.
And the next night.

Open yourself to the power
of the radiant sun by day
and the intense clarity
of one special star each night.
And allow them to recharge you
with their energy and light.

When morning arrives on the third day,
go down to the water's edge
and plunge boldly in.
Sense how
through the silence of your
thought, body, emotions, and spirit,
you have stripped yourself
of all material concerns and desires.
And reintegrated your self
with your god.

Cave fires

See yourself on your inner screen
as you once were.
Outside the enormous cavern,
all is covered by the dark of night.
At the mouth of the cave,
the flames flare upward,
tended by the firewatcher.

You and the others dance together,
in skins stitched by gut thread
into shirt-like shapes
covered with the claws and teeth of creatures
you have shared communion with.

Tribal chants fill the space with
power and light and flashing images
from the gods and the great earth mother.
Silhouetted against the fire,
you and the others whirl and leap
until,
exhausted,
you fall senseless to the ground
and lie together in each others' arms.
You, them, and the gods that be.

The prayer of silence

Until the end of the Middle Ages
and the innovations of St. Ignatius,
this contemplative prayer of silence was
the heart and soul of the Christian tradition.
Involved in the experience are:
A knowledge of God based upon
your own inner love of Him.

And a strong conviction that
the bottom line is
God's faithfulness to you
and not your faithfulness to Him.

This exploration
opens you up to God
in the stillness of your center,
where your will, your intellect,
your emotions, and your god
meet.
This exploration also typifies
the connection between
the essence of prayer and the essence of
complete meditation.

Sit in a straightbacked chair
with your hands separated
and your legs uncrossed and apart.

As you breathe quietly
in and out,
let your awareness drift
to the center of your body,
somewhere between your heart and your abdomen.
Breathe a wave of deep comforting relaxation
directly into your center.
And as you exhale slowly,
allow your breath to carry your tension
down through your hips
and the inner canals of your legs and feet.
And let it out through your toes.
Keep inhaling into your center
and letting your breath and tension
flow out through your toes,
until your lower body is completely relaxed,
heavy, and empty of sensation.

Continue to breathe deeply into your center.
Now, as you exhale,
push your breath and your tension
upwards
through your chest, shoulders, and neck,
and out
through your arms and fingertips.

When your hands are empty and still,
keep inhaling into your center
and pushing all the remaining breath and tension
up through the top of your head
as you exhale.

Soon your body will be silent and still.
So now allow your emotions to surface
and fill the empty space of your body.
Notice them.
Notice all your fear or resistance
or sleepiness or impatience.
And as you continue to breathe rhythmically,
allow your emotions to flow out
on each exhalation.

Then notice your thoughts.
And let them race through you
unchecked and uncensored.
Your mind will seem to be both quiet and active
at the same time.
Allow your favorite selection
from the scriptures to pass through
if you like.
Then review what's happening
in your life today,
including your experiences,
your feelings, your wantings.
And let it all go.
Become aware of how

your thoughts are slowing down
and fading away.
At this point, it won't take long.

Now you are clearly at your center.
Allow yourself to remain there,
untouched by will and imagination.
And expect God to appear.

In the cloud of your unknowing and uncertainty,
you will encounter the roots of prayer.
The responsibility for what happens next
is God's,
not yours.
He can do whatever and go wherever He wants.
So let Him come and touch you.
All you need to do is open the space
for Him to appear.

And when this prayer of silence
is complete for you,
before you open your eyes,
quietly affirm to yourself:
I have loved You with an everlasting love.
I am loved and accepted as I am.
I don't have to do anything or say anything.
He loves me as I am.

Breath meditation

Breath meditation

No one will ever know
whether the whole idea of meditation
evolved out of breath control
and closely-guarded eastern breathing techniques
or whether it was the other way around.
Whichever way it came about,
the two are now just about inseparable.

The three meditative breathing cycles
you have been practicing
are really all you need to achieve
any level of meditation you choose.
But the explorations in this section
will strengthen and reinforce them
as they strengthen and reinforce
your intake and supply of prana
or vital energy from the air.

Prana is said to be the natural energy force
that holds your physical body together
and prevents aging,
muscle atrophy, flab and fat, poor posture,
and other problems involving failing health.
So chances are,
the explorations in this section will
raise your awareness of your breath
and your physical and spiritual energy levels
to new heights.
Just as they've done for untold centuries
of meditators.

Some of the explorations involve
changing your rate of breathing.
Which can be a fascinating experience.
So-called normal breathing
is 16 to 18 breaths per minute.

Ideal normal breathing actually
is more like 11 to 13 breaths per minute.

The faster you breathe,
the less you feel.
Until at 26 breaths per minute
you lose the capacity to feel pain.
Your blood heats up
and your ego shuts down
to the point that all feelings and body sensations
disappear.
Great feats of strength with immunity to being hurt
occur in this state.
But strain and fatigue usually appear later.

Conversely,
the slower you breathe,
the more you feel
and the greater the interaction
between you and the universe.

At ten breaths per minute
for at least a five-minute interval,
your mind becomes clear and ready for work.
The slow steady rhythm
automatically cancels out conflicting thoughts
and inharmonious vibrations around you.
And the effect lasts for hours.

At three even breaths per minute,
the vibratory level of your body becomes
so subdued and harmonized
that all your delicate psychic perceptions
like intuitions, premonitions, and inspirations
come through.
Great creative achievements occur at this level.
And at one long steady breath per minute
for five minutes or more,

the level of concentration you experience is
so intense that the effects
defy description.

Essentially,
increasing your inhalation time and capacity
increases your intake of prana.
Extending the time you hold your inhalation in
allows this vital natural energy
to be completely separated from the air
and stored in your solar plexus.
Lengthening your exhalation time
enables you to make more room for prana
by releasing toxins and impurities in your body
and lets you direct prana
to your storage tanks
or to any part of you that needs it.

Some other explorations in this section
don't focus on your rate of breathing
as much as they focus on
the intensity and depth of your breathing.
Through deeper breathing,
you improve the oxygenation of your blood
and send more pranic nourishment
to every vital organ, endocrine gland,
nerve, muscle, tissue, molecule, and cell
in your body.

So these explorations can literally
help you live longer
and retain your youthfulness and vitality
in addition to
expanding your meditation ability.
And that's the whole point.

You'll experience their benefits most
if you observe the following
ancient yogic breathing meditation rules.

Do them regularly.
Do them after physical exercise, not before.
Do them when you are not excited or breathless.
Do them before meals, never after.
Do them without drinking anything cold afterwards.
Do them and rest or meditate passively afterwards.
Do them cautiously, stopping if you feel faint.
Do them.

Breath

Spontaneous breathing
will hardly seem like an exploration.
But it will lead you to the place
where all explorations begin.

All you have to do is sit still and breathe.
And notice your breath.
That's all.

If you are short of breath when you begin,
notice that.
Don't try to change or lengthen your breath.
Simply notice that it seems short.
And if it begins to lengthen on its own,
notice that.
Don't regulate your breathing.
Don't do anything.
Experience what it's like
just to notice your breath and let it be.

One of three things will happen.

You may begin to feel very sleepy.
And that's good.
Sleepiness is a sign of relaxation.
and if you notice it
and hold onto it

consciously and purposefully
as long as you can,
your sleepiness will pass
into a deeper state of meditation.

You may suddenly notice
lots and lots of thoughts filling your mind
and cluttering your screen
with doubt, impatience, and worries.
That's good too.
Just keep noticing your thoughts
with somewhat detached interest.
Watch them all go by
for as long as you can.
One of them may just turn out to be
an answer that you've been looking for
for years.

You may become so involved with your breathing
that it takes over completely.
And you notice that your breath is
independently alive.
When that happens,
you begin to become your breath.
Nothing exists except your breathing.
Everything is breathing.
And the air is breathing you
as much as you are breathing it.
Well, that's good too.
Because whenever you become one
with your experience,
as you know,
you have entered a state of
complete meditation.
And breathing like this is one way
complete meditation can begin to happen
spontaneously.

Between breath

Sit
in a comfortable position.
Allow yourself to breathe naturally and deeply.
And watch each breath
as it enters and leaves your body.
Notice how your breathing regulates itself
without your having to do anything.

Begin to pay special attention
to the pauses between
each inhalation and exhalation
and again between
each exhalation and inhalation.
Experience these pauses
and allow them to lengthen
all by themselves
by not consciously directing
your next inhalation or exhalation.
And just waiting for it to happen
when it's time for it to happen.

Notice how
just as you think nothing will happen,
something does.
Automatically,
after each pause between breaths,
a new breath flows in
and new life flows on.

You can find infinity
during each pause.
If you look.

Alternate breathing

Every sixty minutes
throughout the day and night
the nostril you inhale through
changes.
And either the right side or the left side
becomes dominant.
Rarely,
except at crossover points,
do you ever breathe through both nostrils
together.

When you breathe through your right nostril,
you become more physical, more active,
more energetic.
Digestion is easier.
Work can be done more effortlessly.
And you feel more assertive and in control.

When you breathe through your left nostril,
you become more spiritual, more passive,
more contemplative.
Daydreams can overtake you.
You feel more spacey and lazy.
And it doesn't matter whether or not
you ever do anything practical again.

When you practice alternate breathing,
you consciously bring both nostrils
into balance.
You process pranic energy more effectively.
And you make it possible to pass
more gently into
complete meditation.

Begin by sitting in your most
comfortable position
but check your spine to be sure it's straight.

Take two or three deep breaths.
And then:

Place the first two fingers of your right hand
just between your eyebrows
on the outside of your screen.
Close your right nostril with your thumb.
And inhale through your left nostril
for four counts.
Close your left nostril with the last two fingers
of your right hand
and hold both nostrils closed for sixteen counts.

Open your right nostril by releasing your thumb
and exhale to the count of eight.

Inhale immediately through your right nostril
to the count of four.
Close both nostrils and hold your breath
for sixteen counts.
Open your left nostril and exhale
for eight counts.

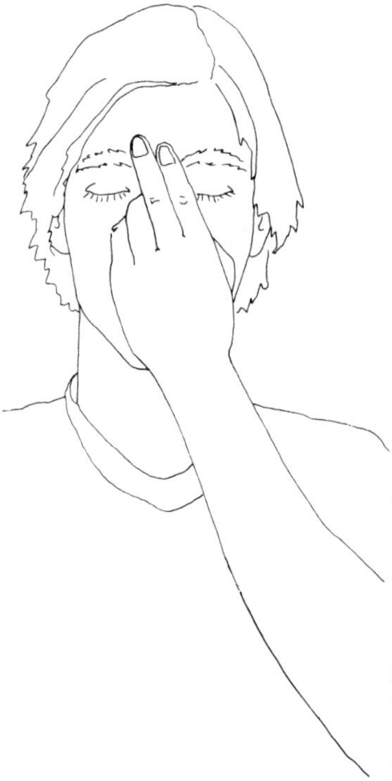

Now close your eyes.
And repeat the entire cycle
two more complete times.
Sense the perfect balance of energy
you are creating
in the left and right sides of your body.
Become aware of
how clear and free from distractions
your mind has become.

If you vary the sequence
to the count of 8:32:16 or 12:48:24
or any other 1:4:2 ratio of counts,
you'll discover
where your own best balance point
can be found.

Vibratory breathing

Sit with your spine straight.
Close your right nostril with your right thumb.
Inhale through your left nostril
and hold your breath
as deep and low in your body as you can.
Then exhale through your left nostril,
making a sound like a large honey bee in May
deep in your throat.
Let the humming sound pervade your consciousness.

Repeat the sequence up to five times
using only your left nostril.
Notice how you slow down and strengthen
your breath.
And how you remove all obstacles to
calmness and concentration.

Sudden shift

Whenever you find it difficult
to shift the rhythm of your breathing
or slow down your breath for meditation,
do this.

Exhale completely,
drawing in your abdomen as far as you can.
Inhale through both nostrils.
And hold.

That's all.

Much later,
when you exhale again,
you will find it easy to shift your breathing
to any pattern, rhythm, or timing you wish.

Freedom breath

If you are still finding it hard
to free your breath
from its automatic and habitual shallowness,
this exploration is the powerful liberator
that you need.

Sit
with your spine straight.
Join the middle and fourth fingers
of your right hand,
straighten them,
and close your left nostril with them.
Stretch your other fingers and thumb backward
and raise your right elbow
until it is level with your shoulder.
Place your left hand on your left knee.

With tremendous force,
breathe in and out through your right nostril
at least ten times.
Then breathe in one more time
and hold your breath as long as you can.
When you need to exhale,
close your right nostril with your thumb,
release your left nostril
and very very slowly exhale through it.

Repeat the cycle three times.
Then reverse nostrils,
using your left hand and arm
in the same position as you had your right.
And repeat the cycle three more times.

Notice the upward movement of your breath.
It will be as free and easy as it used to be
way back when life was a lot simpler
than it appears to be now.

Floating breath

Sit quietly.
Inhale deeply through both nostrils
until your abdomen becomes as bloated
as a big balloon
and looks and feels as if
all the air in your body is being stored there.

See yourself floating gently upward
over any obstacles to your goals
or to your meditation.

Retain the air
and float as long as possible.
Then exhale slowly.
And repeat the cycle as many times as you like.
You'll find it a certain way
to get over any barrier to any objective
that you have been unable to crash through.

Burning breath

Take care with this one.
It will warm you quickly when you are cold
to the point of perspiration.
It will vaporize aging
and keep you feeling light and youthful.
And it will singe away inner distractions
to complete meditation.
But it is a highly advanced yogic technique
that can cause you to pass out
unless you do it absolutely correctly.

Sit on the floor with your legs crossed,
Indian style
and your spine straight.

Close your right nostril with your right thumb
and inhale through your left nostril
slowly and deeply
so that the air fills the entire space
from the base of your spine
to the top of your neck.

Apply force
and hold your breath in
until you feel your face turning red.
Then
close your left nostril
with the third and fourth fingers
of your right hand,
release your right nostril
and exhale through it
just as slowly as you possibly can.

You must exhale with great control
to avoid unconsciousness
and to experience the benefits of this breath.
Do it once only, without reversing it.
And you will see
how powerful
the energy of your breath can be.

Fire breathing

Inhale deeply into your diaphragm.
And exhale.
Inhale again and exhale a little faster.
In and out and in and out again and again,
slowly increasing the tempo each time.
Faster and faster and faster and faster.
In and out.
And in and out and in and out.
And inandoutandinandoutandinandoutandinandoutandinandout.

Send each inhalation to your diaphragm
no matter how short and fast it is
and you will feel your body warming
as your breath becomes a bellows,
fanning the fire deep within you.
And burning away any leftover emotional resistance
to complete meditation.

Withdrawal breath

Anytime you feel harassed
by inner or outer distractions,
this will enable you to withdraw completely.

Sit with your spine straight
and exhale completely.
Then,
close your ears with your thumbs,
close your eyes with your index fingers,
close your nostrils with your middle fingers,
close your lips with your fourth and fifth fingers.

Pull your stomach in
until you sense it almost touching
your backbone.
And concentrate on your inner screen.

When you need to breathe,
lift the middle finger of your left hand
and inhale slowly through your left nostril.
Quickly exhale through your left nostril
without holding your breath.
And replace your finger over the nostril.
Next time you need to breathe,
lift the middle finger of your right hand
and inhale slowly through your right nostril.
Quickly exhale and replace your finger.

Keep shifting nostrils each time you breathe,
for as long as you like.
Remember to draw in your stomach after each inhalation.
And keep watching your screen.

As you withdraw deeper and deeper,
your mind will quiet
and become steady and rippleless.
Your spiritual light will turn on
and you will literally be able to see it.
In the form of
variegated flames and colored lightning bolts
radiating and flashing across your screen.

Centering breath

Sit with your spine straight.
Inhale through both nostrils.
Close your right nostril with your right thumb
and exhale strongly through your left nostril.
Inhale again through both nostrils.
Close your left nostril
with your right index finger
and exhale strongly through your right nostril.
Keep it up
alternating nostrils on each strong exhalation.
Until you notice
that your mind and senses have quieted
and your spiritual center is alive and awake,
in perfect balance and harmony.

Expansion breath

Inhale through both nostrils
and imagine that every cell in your body
is expanding.
Exhale through both nostrils
and imagine that every cell in your body
is retaining its new size
but releasing all toxins and negativity.
Inhale again,
imagining that each cell is expanding even more.
Exhale again,
releasing even more toxins and negativity.
Repeat for at least ten complete breaths
until the space all around
is filled with you.

Active meditation

Active meditation

At the beginning of this book,
you read that anyone can meditate
and it may have sounded global.
But now, you can begin to see
the reason why anyone can meditate is
that everyone is already meditating.
Although everyone may not realize it at the time.

Everyone is meditating
during their alpha transitions
from being awake to being asleep at night
and from sleeping to waking every morning.
And, as you now know,
these are the two most powerful meditative moments
of each day.

Everyone is also meditating
whenever they work, think, exercise,
run, dance, sail, ski, bicycle, skate,
or perform any physical movement over and over
and over and over again
without being preoccupied
with the mechanics or structure
of the movement itself.

Unlike meditating in alpha,
these meditations involve
a shift from the left side of the brain.
Rather than a decrease in
brainwave output.

These activities are active meditations,
another meditative form that needs
no preliminary breathing or positioning work.
And you'll see that until now,
you've been slipping into complete meditation
in a variety of active ways
without fully knowing it.

In this section,
by exploring the way it happens
and noticing how easily and clearly it happens,
you can begin to take charge of
all your active meditation moments.
And enter into them fully
in ways that can enable them
to transform the quality of your life.

Working

If your work involves
performing the same series of motions
again and again throughout the day,
or listening to the same sequence of sounds
again and again throughout the day,
or searching for solutions to the same problem
again and again throughout the day,
you are already aware of the potential problem
of meditating on the job.
At best,
you could space out and lose efficiency.
At worst,
you could cause an accident.

But that's not the way it has to be.

Instead,
you can apply the meditative nature of your work
to the task of
working faster, thinking more clearly,
and finding elusive answers that could get you
a promotion or a raise.
Like this:

At the first moment
you sense that you are drifting into meditation,

lulled by the rhythms of your work
or the stream of your thoughts,
project a picture of yourself onto your screen.

See yourself doing your work
faster, safer, better, more creatively,
and more productively
than you have ever worked before.
Let your picture show you
taking on the role of an ideal worker,
larger than lifesize,
working, thinking, performing in a way
that is a joy to behold.

Hold the image of this picture
for at least a couple of moments.
And watch what happens.
Whatever you do for a living,
this meditation will help you do it better
and get more satisfaction and greater returns
from it.

Exercising

Whenever you exercise,
you are actually creating healthful space
for each cell inside your body
to breathe, grow, thrive,
and contribute to an over-all condition of vitality.
At the same time,
by linking your breath
to a repetitive series of movements,
you are also creating an active gate to
complete meditation.

Jumping rope is a good example of how it works.
As an exercise,
jumping rope increases your endurance,
raises cardiovascular and respiratory efficiency,

strengthens your legs, ankles, and feet,
and improves your coordination, balance,
and sense of being grounded.
As a meditation,
it totally involves you
in a repetitive cycle of coordinated
motion and breath
at a level of concentration
that quickly leads you into meditation.

Use a rope ¼'' to ½'' wide
and long enough for the ends to reach your armpits
when you are standing on the middle.

Start standing
with both feet together,
the middle of the rope lying behind your heels,
and the ends in each hand at thigh level.

With a circular motion of your wrists and arms,
flip the rope over your head
toward the floor in front of you.
Just before it hits,
step over it
one foot at a time,
landing on your toes and the ball of each foot,
and never flatfooted.
When you establish a rhythm,
hook up your breathing.
Inhale as the rope flips up.
Exhale as the rope flips down.

If you count jumpsteps,
you'll feel the meditative effect beginning
somewhere around 25.
The first time you jump rope,
50 is a good place to stop.
Little by little,
you can work your way up to 250 or to 500.

Rest for at least one minute
when you're done.
And stop immediately if you experience
any dizziness or shortness of breath.

Running

Any long distance runner can tell you
about the transcendental moment of opening up
that occurs after running 40 to 45 minutes.
There is no question that the experience is
an active meditation
of the highest order.
It's even called "runner's high."

What happens
is remarkably similar to
what happens
when you meditate with a mantra or a chant.
Through repetition,
whether it be a rhythmic phrase
or a rhythmic stride,
your conscious mind gets tired, shuts down,
and allows other areas of consciousness
to become activated.

In other words,
the repetition of the running mode
like the repetition of Om
shifts your consciousness
from the logical, analytical left side
of your brain
to the intuitive, creative right side
which exists beyond barriers of time and space
in a completely meditative region
of your psyche.

If you are a runner,
you can meditate much more of the time you run
by following three guidelines.

1. Don't compete.
Beating everyone else on the road or sidewalk
or beating your best clock-time
keeps you anchored to the physical side
of running
and prevents excursions into the spiritual side.

2. Run easily.
Meditative running happens
somewhere around the 40-minute mark
no matter what kind of pace you set.
A slow and steady job, a wolf trot,
or an all-out stride
will all take you to the same place
when meditation is your destination.
By running easily,
you can stay a lot longer
when you get there.

3. Turn inward.
Until your meditative shift occurs,
focus your awareness on your breath,
your rhythm, your pain, your sweat,
your pulse and heartbeat.
After your meditative shift occurs,
begin looking outside of yourself
and you'll see the brightest colors
and most emotionally-charged sights you ever saw.

Yoga

A yoga class
that lasts one or two hours
and ends with a deep relaxation
is a classic active meditation in itself.
You can experience the same effect
without the class and without the teacher
when you learn to do the Yoga Salute to the Sun
for 20 to 25 minutes.

The salute to the sun
combines variations of six yoga poses
in a flowing rhythmic sundance
that stretches and relaxes your body
and your mind,
creating a subtle shift into complete meditation.

Begin standing straight
with your feet together,
facing the east if possible.
As you inhale,
visualize the sun just beginning to rise
on the bottom edge of your inner screen.

Exhale.
And bring your palms together at your chest
in a prayerlike position.

Inhale.
Stretch your arms overhead
as you tuck your pelvis slightly forward.
And look up at your hands.

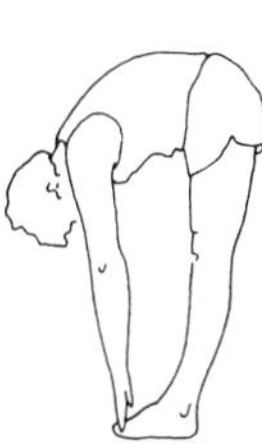

Exhale.
Bend over slowly from your waist
until your hands are touching the floor
in front of or beside your feet.

Inhale.
Lunge forward
by bending your left knee to a right angle
and stepping your right foot back.
Turn your right toes under
and straighten your body from head to heel.

Hold your breath.
Step your left foot back with your toes curled
alongside your right foot
in a push-up position.

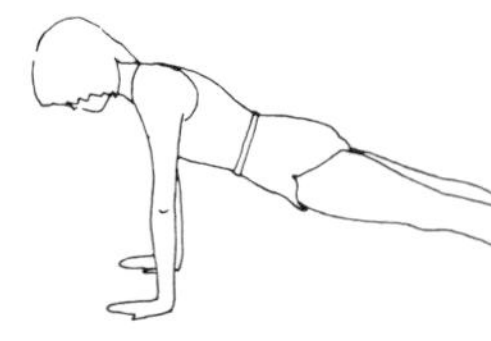

Exhale.
Drop your knees to the floor
and lift your buttocks up.
Then bend your elbows,
bringing your chest and chin to the floor.
Continue exhaling.
And lower your whole body to the floor.
Straighten your legs,
but keep your toes curled under.

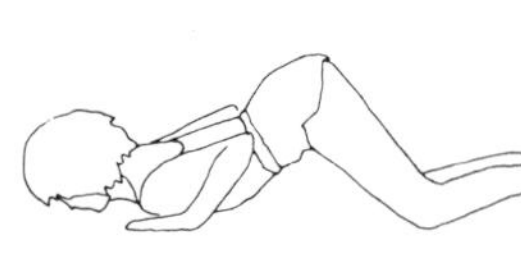

Inhale.
Push down on your hands and slowly lift your head
as you straighten your elbows.
Arch upward slowly
as a cobra arches upward before it strikes.

Exhale.
Lift your buttocks all the way up
and keep your head down,
forming a pyramid.

Inhale.
Lunge forward
by bending your right knee
and stepping your right foot forward
between your hands.

Exhale.
straighten your right leg
and bring your left foot next to your right.
Lift your buttocks high
until you're in a standing bend again.

Inhale.
Slowly lift your spine
by unrolling it one vertebra at a time.
Lift your head last.
Look up, raise your arms straight overhead.
And allow the image of the rising sun
to form again on your screen.

Exhale.
Bring your arms slowly down to your sides,
allowing your image to become
brighter and brighter.

Repeat the salute to the sun
at least six times.
And over the course of a week or two,
gradually extend it to 24 repetitions.

Done quickly,
these sun poses are yoga's answer to jogging.
Done slowly,
they are deeply and powerfully relaxing.
Either way,
once you smooth out the rhythm,
coordinate each step with your breath,
and move gracefully as if dancing,
you'll greet the sun each day
with a complete meditation.

Tai chi

What yoga is to Indian monks and meditators,
tai chi is to Chinese Taoists.
In a 15 to 25 minute form that includes
between 60 and 150 free-flowing,
yet totally integrated movements and weightshifts,
you move slowly
with grace and precision
as if in an underwater ballet

You move so slowly
that you have time to be fully aware of
all the details that make up each movement
as well as your relationship to gravity,
the air, and the space all around you.

You move so slowly
that everything just sort of happens
and you are completely involved
in the flow of each movement
as it happens.

All the while,
you concentrate your life force
in your solar plexus,
strengthening it there,
and then allowing it to permeate
your entire body.

Each step
focuses your awareness
in the present moment of existence
as if you were a single entity
living only here and only now.

All together
the tai chi form
fuses your mind and body and breath

into the harmony of oneness
and complete meditation.

You can get an idea of how it works
with this simple tai chi lift.

Stand
with your feet at shoulder width,
your pelvis tucked under you
so that your spine is straight,
your knees bent forward slightly
so they are almost directly over your feet,
and your toes turned outward
at a 45-degree angle to your body.

Let your shoulders and elbows relax
and exhale,
lifting your wrists
and allowing them to carry your
forearms, elbows and upper arms along
behind them.
When both forearms are parallel to the floor
and your hands are dangling loosely
from your wrists,
inhale.
Lift your hands and fingers
until they are straight-line extensions
of your forearms and wrists,
with your palms facing the floor.

Now begin to exhale slowly.
Allow all your weight to begin to shift
onto your right leg.
Notice that your right leg is carrying
one-hundred percent of you
and that your left leg feels light.
As your left leg continues to lighten,
lift your heel and inhale.
Then lifting from the knee,

bring your left knee up to your left hand
with your toes pointing to the floor.
As you exhale very slowly,
allow gravity to float your left leg
back to the floor.

Stay on the same horizontal line,
keep exhaling,
and slowly push your weight off your right leg
and onto your left leg.
Feel your left leg grow heavier.
Feel your right leg grow lighter.
Imagine water flowing out of one leg
and into the other.
When all the water is in your left leg,
allow your right heel to lift.

Inhale.
And lifting from the knee,
let your right knee rise
to meet your right hand,
bringing the lower part of your leg
dangling along behind it.
After you notice the lightness,
exhale
and give gravity permission
to float your right foot slowly to the floor.
Then equalize your weight once again.

You may keep shifting your weight
and lifting
slowly.
Back and forth, back and forth.
As many times as you like.

Become aware
of each muscle stretching and contracting
as you shift your weight.

Become aware
of how connected to the ground
your heavy leg is each time.

Become aware
of the rhythm of your motion
and your breath.
Become aware
of the gentle meditative state
drifting over you.
And stay with it all the way into
complete meditation.

Dancing

Movement and music meshing together
can carry you into meditation
whenever you dance alone.
Turn on some music when you are all alone.
Something soft and flowing.
Or something with a hard driving beat.
Be.
By yourself.
Stand quietly and really hear the music.
Let the sound surround you,
breathe to its rhythm,
and enter into it.
When you and the music are one,
begin to move.

Riding on the crest of the music,
let yourself move freely.
Keep breathing deeply into your diaphragm.
Sense your body as you move.
Sense, especially, your pelvis.
And let it go.

Move in ways you may never have moved before.
Notice how awkward uncoordinated movements
flow into graceful and meditative
new experiences
as you maintain your oneness
with the music.

Afterward,
sit in your favorite meditation position
for a few minutes.
And watch what happens.

Playing

If you ski or sail or bicycle or roller skate
or involve yourself in any outdoor activity
that does not involve teamwork or competition,
you may already be aware of
the wide open meditative gate
you can enter
just for fun.

Whatever the experience is,
whether you're carving turns with hard-biting edges
or rocking gently on the waves and the breeze
or pushing off and just rolling along,
when you stay in the essence of it
without worrying about technique,
rightness, or winning,
you will quickly pass beyond yourself.
And actively enter into
complete meditation.

Whirling

Whirling is an excellent active meditation
in itself.
It's also an active meditation block remover
when you're having trouble getting into it.

Begin by standing
in your meditative star pose.
Shift all your weight
onto the ball of your right foot
and allow it to become a stationary pivot point.
Then, with your eyes open
and your body moving as one connected whole,
push off your left foot
and whirl or spin your body with outstretched arms
in a clockwise direction.

Whirl slowly and rhythmically.
Without attempting to focus your eyes
on any single spot.
Keep breathing deeply,
at the rate of one breath per revolution.

Start with only seven whirling revolutions
and work your way up to
as many as you like.
When you finish,
to avoid losing your balance and falling,
look straight ahead and breathe deeply
until your stability returns.

Because the earth rotates from West to East,
whirling in a clockwise mode
or from the East or left side of your body
to the West or right side of your body,
balances you, relaxes you, and gives you
an active voice in the polarizations and motions
of the planet.
Dervishes whirl for hours
in religious meditation marathons.
The same technique can help you meditate completely.
Just give it a whirl.

Other external gates

Wherever you are,
you can always discover a nearby active gate
into meditation.
When you know what to look for,
access to a meditation break
will be close at hand
no matter how busy, noisy, empty, still, or mixed
your space is.

For instance,
if you let your vision tunnel in
and concentrate fully and single-pointedly on
the sight or the sound of cars going by,
crickets chirping or peepers peeping,
waves rolling, rippling, or crashing in,
a vacuum cleaner's drone in the next room,
typewriters typing,
people passing by a window,
ants walking,
leaves rustling,
ambience humming in an empty room,
or any repetitive or constant
external motion or sound,
you will shift almost effortlessly
within minutes or maybe less
into a completely meditative state of mind.
And you will come back to wherever you were
one to twenty minutes later,
feeling better, clearer, more vital,
more energized,
and more able to handle the events of your life
than you were before.

Energizing meditation

Energizing meditation

As a physical creature,
your life is literally a subtly shifting balance
between matter or mass
and energy.
At any given moment,
you are actively involved in the process
of converting elemental energy sources
into cellular material and body tissue
and converting cellular material and body tissue
back into elemental energy sources.

By consciously accelerating and expanding
this natural process through meditation,
you begin to enter into realms of
the yogi's kundalini,
the Taoist's chi or hara,
and the Star War jedi's Force.
They are all one and the same.
And they are all the stuff
from which miracles and universes are made.

When you energize yourself
at a reasonably high level of efficiency,
you feel good.
You experience a fundamental sense of harmony.
And your joy is only occasionally punctuated
by upsets.

When you don't energize yourself
at a reasonably high level of efficiency,
the opposite is true.
You feel uncentered and alienated.
And the upsets in your life
consistently outweigh the joy.

Complete meditation
automatically heightens your capacity
to energize
by emphasizing deep diaphragmatic breathing
and eliminating all distractions
from your field of focus.

The explorations in this section
direct you to many of the outer and inner sources
of available energy.
And show you how to tap into them.

As you add them to your beginning explorations
that take you down to alpha
on your breath, body position, or mantra,
they give you a choice of complete meditations
designed to fill you with extra vitality
and well-being.
And to keep you that way.

The elements

Ancient meditators from all human cultures
had the power, knowledge, and wisdom
to directly command the forces of
earth, air, fire, and water.
They could see and participate with
elves and gnomes of the earth,
sylphs and fairies of the air,
transparent spirits of the fire and light,
and sprites and undines of the water.
This ability is the fabric
of many surviving myths.

The fact is
these elemental forces are still all around.
And still able to heal, help, purify,
and revitalize you.

To connect with their essences,
put yourself in tune with nature
from a completely meditative point of view.

Air.
Walk in the country
or see yourself walking in the country
on your inner screen.
Breathe deeply
and sense the elementals of the air
that revive you and refresh you.

Earth.
Sit in a field of flowers or a garden
or see yourself there on your screen.
And let your consciousness reach out
toward the forces of life
and growth and beauty
that radiate from the abundant earth.

Fire.
Close your eyes in warm bright sunlight
or in front of a crackling fire.
Then partially open your eyes
and sense the almost transparent
dancing, hovering patterns of light
carrying the healing sensations of fire
to you.

Water.
Consider the water
that bathes every cell in your body
and all cellular life on your planet.
All life emerged from a single primordial sea.
And the waters of your ancestry
still flow around you
in body fluids, ponds, streams, rivers,
oceans, arctic ice fields, and summer clouds.

There is an incredible and indescribable power
in nature that's manifested through the elements.
It is there for your enrichment and enjoyment.
Whenever you enter into it through
complete meditation.

Chakras

Chakra is an old Sanscrit word
that means wheel.
It describes the circular, spiraling
fields of energy
radiating in or just beyond your body.

Traditionally and historically,
seven chakras have been identified
and written about.

Each was linked to one of the seven
then-known planetary energy systems.
Today, we know there are more than seven planets.
And there are more than seven chakras.

CHAKRA	1	2	3	4	5	6	7	8	9	10	11	12	13	
NOTE	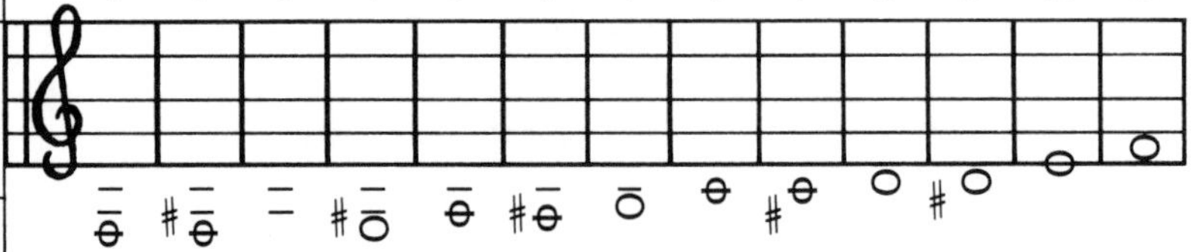													
NAME	**Root**	**Illium**	**Sacral**	**Splenic**	**Solar**	**Heart**	**Chest**	**Throat**	**Jaw**	**Brow**	**Ring**	**Crown**	**Outer**	
LOCATION	Coccyx	Pelvic Joints	Abdomen	Spleen Naval	Solar Plexus	Heart	Upper Chest, Shoulders	Neck	Jaw hinge	Forehead, third eye	Hands Elbows Knees Wrists Ankles Feet	Top of Head	2'-4' above head	
RULER	Earth	Vulcan	Pluto	Jupiter	Mars	Sun	Venus	Mercury	Chiron	Moon	Saturn	Uranus	Neptune	
SYMBOL	⊕	¥	♇	♃	♂	☉	♀	☿	⚷	☽	♄	♅	♆	
RULES	Material needs	Service	Sex, Trans-formation	Expansion health	Action, Power, Assertion	Body/ mind vitality	Creativity love, self expression	Commun-ication intellect	Teaching healing	Psyche, sub-conscious change	Discipline Focus, Duty	Breaking free	Spirit, illusion	
COLOR	Green	Bronze	Red	Pink, Lavender	Orange	Gold	Brass	Yellow	Blue	Indigo	Gray	**Purple**	White	
GLAND	—	—	Ovaries Glands	Spleen pancreas liver	Adrenal	Thymus	Pituitary	Thryoid	—	Pituitary	Para-Thryoids	Pineal	—	

In and around your own body,
you can discover and contact
thirteen major chakras.
And there are probably
at least a hundred or more minor ones.

Most of your key chakras
are located along the path
from the base of your spinal column
to the top of your head.
And, with one exception, they radiate
from the cerebral-spinal column,
major organs, or major joints,
as you can see in the illustration.

All minor chakras radiate
from each joint connecting your bones.
The most readily identifiable ones
are bunched together in your hands and feet
where you have more bones per square inch
than anywhere else in your body.

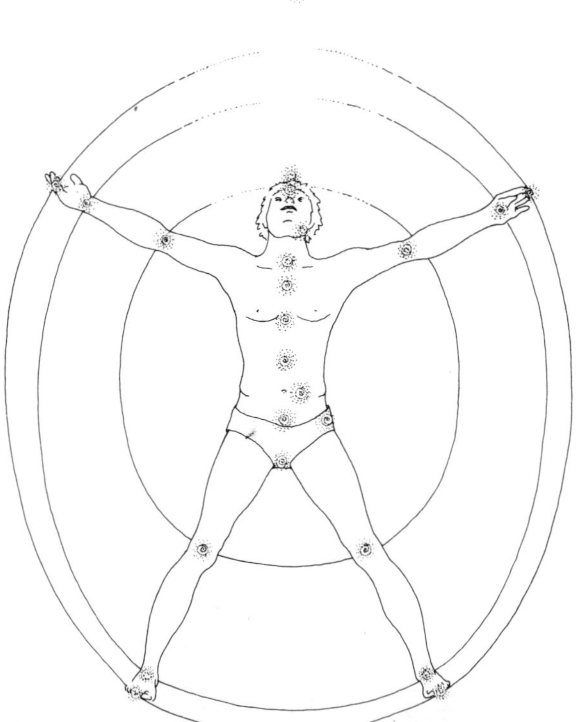

You can feel them
just by holding your hands
a couple of feet apart
and slowly bringing them together
until you feel a magnetic kind of resistance.

That's chakral energy
from a lot of small chakras all acting
together.
And each of the major chakras
is infinitely more powerful than that.

The lower ones,
including your root, pelvic, sacral, solar,
and splenic chakras
are involved with physical and emotional planes.
Your heart, upper chest, throat and ring chakras
relate to developing awareness
of forces beyond the self.
Your jaw, brow, crown and outer chakras
awaken only through spiritual evolution
and enlightenment.

Opening chakral paths before you are ready
is said to produce a loss of balance
in your personal energy, emotions, and health.
But generally,
anyone who chooses to put the time and effort
into awakening chakras
is already ready.
And natural chakral blocks usually prevent
premature opening.

For example,
if you are still locked up
in incomplete first chakra material issues,
unresolved third chakra sexual conflicts,
or angry fifth chakra power struggles,
your heart chakra will not be available to you.

You usually discover that your path to the higher chakras
is blocked
wherever you are blocked in your own experience.

In the explorations that follow,
you can begin to connect meditationally
with your chakras
and the colors, sounds, and energies
that influence them.
These explorations are perfectly safe to work with.
They incorporate self-limiting fuses
that enable you to go for your own energy limits
at any given time.
Without overloading your circuits.

Auras

Auras are visible energy fields
that surround every living creature.
Kirlian photography reveals them
as biophysical energy emissions.
What they are, in fact, are
outward manefestations of inner chakral energy
that reveal which chakras are dominant
at any given time
and what kind of shape their energy is in.

Each person's aura
can vary in color over the entire spectrum
and in size from a few wispy inches
to waves or rays extending many feet
beyond the body.
It all depends on an individual's
health, emotional mood, and spiritual evolution.

Meditation will awaken your ability
to see the auras of people around you.
Which will introduce you gently
to the way chakras work.

It's really very simple.
So simple that it demonstrates
the ancient saying:
Widen your field of vision
and you'll see more of what's in front of you.

You see,
auras are already there.
Plain as noses on faces.
If you don't see them,
it's only because you're looking right past them
or around them or through them.
So here's how to notice and interpret them.

Begin by working with a friend.
Sit your friend a few feet in front of you
against a white or plain-colored wall.
And have a lamp projecting a lot of light on her.

Sit yourself in a comfortable meditation position.
Close your eyes
and breathe a few easy deep meditation breaths.
Then slowly open your eyes.
And look deeply into your friend's eyes.
Maintaining eye contact,
allow your field of peripheral vision to expand.
Extend your focus
to include the space that surrounds
your friend's head.

Continue breathing slowly and deeply
and become aware of the field of color
that fills the space.
Don't try to see it.
Just notice that it's there,
in the extended range of your vision.
And take in its size and color.

A red aura
is a sign of physical vitality and sexuality.

Orange and gold
indicate highly energized self direction.

Yellow
is a sign of intellectual and mental activity.

Green
shows balance, harmony, and peacefulness.

Blue
signifies a state of inspiration or spirituality.

Indigo, violet, and purple
are signs of psychic development and mysticism.

Dull mottled colors
in wisps close to the head and body
are general indications of low energy, unrest,
ill health, or the negative expression
of a bright color's positive attribute.
Brightness and whiteness
extended outward in brilliant waves or rays
show highly evolved awareness and consciousness.

Once you get the idea,
you won't need lighting or props
or even eye contact
to see auras.
Wherever you go,
you'll only have to imagine yourself
in a meditative state
and selectively open your field of vision
to include the aura of anyone you're with.

You can even see your own aura
by connecting with your own eyes
in a large mirror
and expanding your field of focus
to include the space around your head.

In this manner,
you can monitor the condition of your vitality.
And watch your aura brighten and grow
along with your ability to enter into
complete meditation.

Colors

Seeing auras
begins to reawaken your sensitivity
to the power of color
as an energizing, healing, and meditative force.
From your own state of meditation,
you can draw upon color
to enrich and to alter the direction of your life.
Like this:

Choose the color you want to work with.
Usually the first one you think of
is the one you need.
So stay with that one.

Then,
after you have entered meditation
and after your breath has settled itself
in a slow, deep, steady rhythm,
as you inhale,
begin to visualize a small cloud
colored exactly like your color
forming about 18 inches above your head.

As you exhale,
sense that the cloud floats down,
surrounding your head and shoulders
and drifting into and through your body.

Each time you inhale,
recreate the cloud above your head.
Each time you exhale,
allow the cloud to drift down
and surround you with its color.
A cycle of 21 complete breaths
will take you completely into your color
and your color completely into you.

Remember:
Green restores, regenerates, and balances.
Red strengthens vitality and sexuality.
Pink purifies.
Orange energizes.
Gold warms.
Yellow stimulates mental activity.
Blue cools and inspires.
Indigo, violet, and purple expand psychic ability.
White protects and raises consciousness.
You can match each color to its chakra
by referring back to the chart on page 124,
and use this exploration
to contact, strengthen, and reinforce
each of your chakral energy fields.

Sound

Sounds, like colors,
relate to specific chakras
as well as to the way
you harmonize with or clash against
your environment.

Through prehistory,
sound has been used to influence crops,
alter the weather, heal illnesses,
enhance learning skills,
and change emotional moods.

At its simplest level,
that's why some music brings you up
while other music shuts you down.
And while rhythm reinforces the effect,
the primary power is in the sound.
When they tell you
"In the beginning was the word,"
what they're talking about is the sound
of creation.

Just as each of your key chakras
has a color or energy ray all its own,
each vibrates to its own musical note or tone.

There are two interesting things about this.
First is that
chakral tones are relative and not absolute.
They vary from person to person
and from day to day.
So while they always have
the same pitch relationships to one another,
they don't always begin on the same tone.
Second is that
whenever two or more people hum or chant together,
each of their relative chakral notes
for each chakra
will merge into one note
exactly the way that a group of pendulums
swinging at the same rhythm
will always end up all swinging
in the same direction,
no matter how they begin.

You can tune into the music of your chakras
using musical notation
if you have a piano or play an instrument.
If you don't,
you can still tune in easily by ear.

Turn back to the chakra diagram on page 124,
and note the numbers of each key chakra
and its approximate location in your body.

The lowest note you reach for
when you sing the word "my"
in "My Country 'Tis Of Thee"
is the note that will start
your first or root chakra
resonating.
Try it.
Just hum the note deep inside
where you sense your coccyx to be,
or sing the word "Om" to it.

The note in between the first chakra note
and the next note in a do-re-mi scale
is the note for your second chakra.
If you sing "do. . . re. . . "
and slide down from "re" to a note
between the two,
that's it.
Try it.
And notice a resonating pulsing
in your pelvic joints,
right where both of your thigh bones connect.

Moving up by half tones
through the chromatic scale, as it is called in music,
you can connect with each of your chakras
as they appear on the chart.
Remember to hum
or to sing Om,
drawing it out in a long hummed Ommmmmmmmmmmm.

Try each note
sliding pitch by pitch
all the way up the scale.
And notice where the inner fluttering responses are
in your body.

That response is how it feels
when your chakras awaken for you
under your own direction.

At the top of the scale,
you reach the note for your outer chakra,
that's two to four feet above your head
and your direct line to the universe.
Hold the note,
letting the sound rise in pitch
in your throat and head
like a soft wailing siren,
as you experience the part of you
that is also a part of
the all that is.

After you practice
linking up the sounds and the chakra responses,
add one slowly ascending chromatic chakra scale
to your meditation cycle each day.
Sense your energy flowing upward
with each sound.
And become aware of the way
each chakral area becomes fully relaxed
and fully energized at the same time.
As you turn it on.

If you experience
some of your chakras responding less easily
than others,
remembering that the higher chakras only open up
when energy is flowing freely
through the lower ones.
It's somewhat of an evolutionary process.

Tune in on the lowest chakra
that you have difficulty
getting a response from.

And for five minutes,
breathe meditatively and concentrate
on the color, its sound, and its location.
Usually two or three five-minute probes like this
will weaken the block
and allow a response to flutter through.

Planetary energies

Each of your chakras is also in tune,
in resonance and in harmony
with a specific planet.
In this respect as in astrology,
the Sun and Moon are classified as planets.
And the recently acknowledged planetoid Chiron
and a yet-to-be-acknowledged planet Vulcan
are included as governing chakral influences.

Each segment of this exploration
can become a separate meditation of its own.
Or all the segments may be used,
like sounds or with sound and colors,
to connect all your chakras
in an expansive and free-flowing pattern.

In each case,
see the planetary symbol on your screen,
let your awareness flow into
the location of the corresponding chakras.
And repeat the planetary affirmation
as many times as you like.

Chakra 1. Earth.
I have what I need.
And as I need more, I have more.

Chakra 2. Vulcan.
I work for what I want.
And my work sustains me.

Chakra 3. Pluto.
I am strong and sexual.
And my creatureness is the source
of my transformation.

Chakra 4. Jupiter.
I am surrounded by expansive abundance
and filled with the health and wealth
of the universe.

Chakra 5. Mars.
I have enormous power and intensity
and I am willing and able to act on it.

Chakra 6. Sun.
I am the essence and the source
of a glowing vitality that fills my life
with warmth and love.

Chakra 7. Venus.
I express myself freely, creatively,
and lovingly throughout the universe,
and I am loved in return.

Chakra 8. Mercury.
I communicate openly and honestly
with beacon-like intellectual clarity
and insight.

Chakra 9. Chiron.
I share my experience and participate,
teaching and healing with compassion.

Chakra 10. Moon.
I journey without fear
through the landscapes of my psyche
and return with all the hidden powers I possess.

Chakra 11. Saturn.
I overcome each limitation in my path
with disciplined focus and understanding.

Chakra 12. Uranus.
I break free,
spontaneously changing form and structure
into the substance of the universe.

Chakra 13. Neptune.
I enter illusion,
drifting into it and beyond,
a being of pure energy.

Complete chakral energizing

Stand
in your star pose.
Breathe yourself gently
into a near meditative state.
And feel in the trunk of your body
for the place where your heart chakra is.

There have been gradual shifts
in chakral energy
over the course of this century,
a movement upward
from the traditional center of the body
in the solar chakra
toward the heart.
By beginning this exploration
centered in your heart chakra,

you can accelerate an evolutionary step
that will bring humanity into
the Aquarian Age.

Move into your heart chakra
and sound its note.
If you don't read music,
you can find it by humming the notes
of the NBC station break chimes,
starting on as low a note as you can.

You'll find your heart chakra
on the same note as the "C."
Allow one full breath for this note
and wait for the response before moving on.
Move down the scale one chromatic tone
to find your solar chakra,
and allow another complete breath.
When you connect, move two tones up
to your chest chakra,
breathing, humming, and moving down
in a widening circle
to the next note and the next chakra.

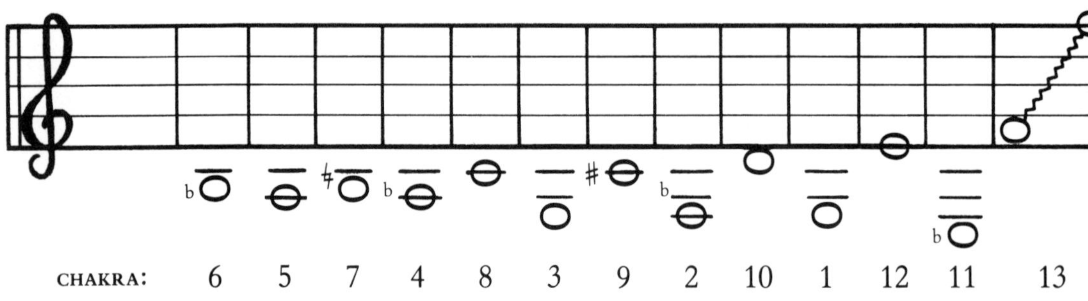

What you are doing
is moving up and down the musical scale
in everwidening gaps
which take in each chakra
in an outwardly spiraling path.

Because the notes of the scale
are chromatic half tones
or the smallest interval
that the average ear can distinguish
between notes,
you can easily tune in to each chakra in turn
by sliding up and down the scale out loud
and counting notes
until you hit the right one.
And then by confirming the rightness
of that note
by checking the location
of the area in your body
where you begin to feel a fluttering response.

As you focus on your heart chakra and its note
at the beginning,
and see it as the center vortex
of a whirlpool of energy
that extends outward in everwidening circles,
you re-create the pattern of the universe
note by note and chakra by chakra,
as you follow the musical pattern.

In effect,
your chakras awaken
in a much more natural pattern
than the traditional straight-line one.
Ripples, atoms and molecules, solar systems,
nebulae, and galazies all flow
in the same spiraling shape.

If you begin your meditations
whirlpooling and flowing outwardly
from your heart chakra
to your ring and outer chakras
and widen the circles in a clockwise motion,
you can enter into each meditation
fully empowered and fully energized.

If you end your meditations
whirlpooling and flowing inwardly
from your outer and ring chakras
to your heart chakra,
closing the circles in a clockwise motion,
you can return from each meditation
in complete harmony
with all the spiraling energy patterns
of self, nature, and universe.

Just follow the musical notes
and notice when the notes connect.
It sounds a lot more complicated
than it actually is.
And as you'll discover, the benefits
and the enlightenment you can experience
are well worth exploring.

Mental meditation

Mental meditation

Many people who have never meditated
will probably tell you
as they see you carrying this book around,
that meditation is impractical,
almost as lazy and shiftless as daydreaming,
and definitely not for them.

You,
if you choose,
can simply nod, smile, and move along.
Because, as you know,
meditation is indeed for everyone
whether they acknowledge it or not.
And meditation is indeed an advanced form
of daydreaming.
But there's nothing wrong with that.

In this section
you will begin to discover
that in addition to being
relaxing, centering, and energizing,
meditation is also immensely practical.
It can be used to
accelerate the traditional process of learning,
improve your memory,
involve you in an automatic source of knowledge,
provide you with a direct line
to creative ideas and inspiration,
and put you in touch with mental powers
that can help you on a lifelong basis.
Starting now.

Mental clearing

After you have entered alpha
in your favorite meditation position,
and your breathing is slow and deep,
this ancient yoga chant will increase
your mental and intellectual receptivity
to new material of any kind.

Say aloud or silently
to yourself:
Ohm-mah-nee-pahd-may-hoom
Ohm-mah-nee-pahd-may-hoom
Ohm-mah-nee-pahd-may-hoom
Say it over and over for three to five minutes.
And allow the vibrations of the chant
to massage the inner area of your head.

When you're done,
you'll be ready
for any learning or mental activity
you have to do.
Including the other explorations
in this section.

Try this mental clearing chant
whenever you experience a meditation block.
It enables your stream of consciousness
to flow at the rate of
one slow-motion picture at a time.
And leaves you completely calm and clear.

Accelerated learning 1

Enter your meditative state
with the book or reference notes
that you are learning from
at your side.

When you are in complete meditation,
mentally clear, alert, and receptive,
open your eyes and start reading.
At first,
read for only five to ten minute periods.
Later you can lengthen your learning time.

When you have finished reading,
close your eyes and re-enter
complete meditation.
Gently suggest to yourself
that you will remember everything
you have read.
Because there has been no conflict of attention,
you will.
Whatever you take in this way
leaves a deep and lasting imprint
and becomes available for total recall
exactly the way you have implanted it.

Accelerated learning 2

Use your waking-to-sleeping alpha period
each night
to program your ability to absorb data
while you are asleep.
Place a book or pages from a notebook
under your pillow.
Be sure that the material is opened
to the part you want to learn.
As you drift into sleep,
hold your alpha line
long enough to tell yourself that
you will learn the material under your pillow
before morning
and have it available for recall
whenever you wish.

Repeat your intention three times
as you visualize the material under your pillow
on your screen.
Then sleep on it.

When you awake,
you will have it all.
This exploration worked for Edgar Cayce
when he was a schoolboy
with a learning problem.
And it will work for you.

Memory tapes

Make a cassette recording
of anything you want to memorize.
Like a list, a system, words to a song,
a part in a play, a speech,
or anything else.
Record your tape is a deep resonant voice
that comes from your diaphragm or your heart.
Raise your voice slightly
to accent or underline anything important.

If there is room on your tape,
record what you want to learn over again
to fill your tape to the end.

Then enter into
complete meditation
with your cassette player at your side.
When you are in your meditative state,
push the button that turns your tape on.
Be sure that you have pretuned your player
to a moderately low volume.
And just listen.

Notice the rhythm of your voice.
See the content of your words on your screen.
And know that you are entering
what's on your cassette tape
onto your memory tape
like an auditory Xerox machine.

A few sessions will make it clear to you
that memories are made of this.

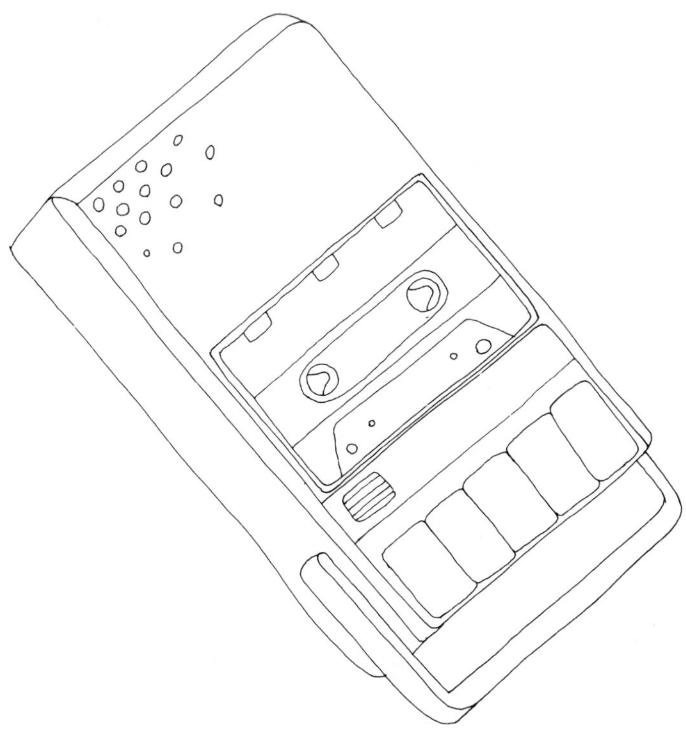

Knowing

If you've ever just known something
without studying to know it,
working at knowing it,
or looking for ways to know it,
then you already have an idea of what
this exploration is all about.

Knowing,
the condition where material comes to you
automatically and effortlessly,
begins with not knowing.
In other words,
when you know
that you don't know
something that you want to know,
complete meditation
will enable what you want to know
to come to you.

As you'll soon see, it works.
Whether you use it to find
a simple answer
or an entire body of scientific information.
But it works easiest for you
when you accept
two almost unacceptable principles.
And then proceed to apply them.

Principle 1.
Everything there is to know is already known
and on file.
Either in your own cells, psyche, or subconscious.
Or in a place that's easily accessible
to them and to you.
Traditional occult people call this place
the Akashic Records, the one-mind and the collective unconscious.
But this place is really you and yours.

Principle 2.

There are no exceptions to the first principle.
It's in the area of application
that problems come up.
And in this respect,
allowing the process of knowing to occur
can be as difficult for you
as allowing the process of seeing to occur
would be
for someone who had always walked around
with his eyelids tightly closed.

But this exploration will help.

Enter complete meditation
with the question you want the answer to,
the subject you want information about,
or the type of knowledge you want to know
in clear visual focus on your inner screen.

Create the words of the question or subject
in sharply chiseled golden letters,
without thinking mentally about them.
And hold them on your screen in perfect clarity
for at least ten seconds
before you let them fade.

Then allow your next thoughts or pictures
to come to you
without judging, criticising, or evaluating them.
And watch them play across your screen.

Take what you get.
And see where it takes you.
Even if it doesn't seem to be
exactly what you asked for,
in the beginning,
just leave it alone.

You may get an obvious answer right away.
You may get immediate symbols for the answer
that need to be thought about
and translated into words and concepts later.
Or you may have to flip through
racks of file folders
that you're not used to
finding your way around in,
to get the information that you're seeking.

But you will get it,
automatically,
by just allowing it to surface.
Because it's already there,
all you need to do is let it out.

Advanced knowing

Sometimes you probably get the sensation
that there is something you need to know.
And that if you only knew it,
problem areas of your life would begin
to clear up.
Whenever you don't know
exactly what you need to know,
try this.

Enter complete meditation
with a sharply chiseled golden question mark
on your inner screen.
And hold a thought formed around the notion that
there is something you need to know
right now.
Bring your question mark into brilliant focus.
Then let it dissolve.

Once again,
take what you get without being self critical.
What you get is what you need to know.

In essence,
you are shifting gears
to a higher internal source of knowledge
than your mind.
Your higher source knows
what you need to know.
And all your life,
it has put what you need to know
indirectly in your path or in your thoughts.

The only difference now
is that you're going directly and consciously
to your source.

If you discover that you seem to keep losing
what you learn
as you leave your state of complete meditation,
implant the suggestion
that you will remember whatever comes up
whenever you want.
Naturally, you will.

Creative inspiration and invention

Like knowledge,
creative ideas, scientific inventions,
themes for artistic and musical works,
and all kinds of other inspirational material
are all available to you
in unlimited quantities.

Without knowing it,
you've used this universal pool
of creative inspiration and invention
many times already.
Every time you've ever had
an original idea,

a sudden beautiful thought,
or a breakthrough concept,
this is where you got it.

Knowing that,
you can have a whole lot more of it
now.
All you have to do is ask for it
when you enter
complete meditation.

Specifically:
After you are
in a comfortable meditation position,
and your breath is flowing deeply in your body,
and your mind is clear and still,
and you are crossing over into alpha
open up your inner screen
to new ideas or creative inspiration.
And see what you get.

What comes up will usually be
ideas you can use at work,
poems, songs, art and pottery objects
you can make,
and things like that.
But as you develop and work with
your ability to tap into your creative source,
you can find some truly wonderful gifts there.
Like
playing a musical instrument instantly by ear,
painting without lessons and without numbers,
a better singing voice,
a new mathematical formula,
tomorrow's version of the safety pin,
or anything else you'd like
to enrich and expand the creativity of your life.

Contacting your inner guides

Some of your meditative work in this section
may go easier for you
if you choose this point in time
to connect with your inner guides.

These entities are available to you
as you begin to probe
the yet unexplored realms of your psyche.
Like any guides,
they can make your meditative journeys
simpler and more direct
because they know the shortest paths
to your inner goals.
Like any teachers,
they can focus your efforts
on the most productive channels open to you.

Your guides are already there.
In your psyche or just beyond.
Some call them psychic entities
or ghosts from other planes.
But where they really come from
are past or future versions of
you or your spiritual essence
in other physical or non-physical forms
in time and space.
Here is how to contact them.

Choose a time or a day
when you really want to meet your guides.
And enter into complete meditation
with that intent.

When you are over the line into alpha
with a perfectly clear inner screen,
without thinking any further about it

snap the picture of the first male figure
who comes mind
onto your screen.
He may be from any historical period.
Past, present, future,
long before recorded history or beyond.
But the first man you meet in this mode
is one of your inner guides.
So ask him his name
and any other questions you may have.

Then ask him to wait a moment,
right where he is.
And snap a picture of the first female figure
who comes to mind
onto your screen beside him.
Ask her for her name.
And ask any other questions you may have.

Quite possibly,
your male and female guides
will not come to you
from the same historical periods.
And they may or may not share
the same skills and aptitudes.
Nevertheless,
they will come to you from this point on.
Use your guides
whenever you need them.
Both in and out of
complete meditation.
They will support your expansiveness
in long range ways
that will greatly benefit
your learning experiences right now.
And many of your explorations still to come.

Healing meditation

Healing meditation

Complete meditation
can enable you to regain and maintain
as perfect a condition
of health, energy, and vitality
as you are willing to let yourself
claim, have, and keep.

For this to happen,
it's important to take in
what makes it work.
And how you can make it work for you.

As a race and as a culture,
we have allowed ourselves to become unconscious
about the nature of nature
and the nature and purpose of our lives.
The fact is:
You
and everything you were, are, and will be
are a basic intersection
of spirit and flesh,
joined together
along a series of single points
in time and space.
Each single point is now,
the moment that you are experiencing.
Together,
all these single points connected
form the lifeline of your life.

At each of these single points
along the continuum of your life,
you use the energy of your spirit to create
the form and matter of your body.
And you use the form and matter of your body
to replenish the energy of your spirit.

In these terms,
your physical body is
the temple, sanctuary, and laboratory
of your spirit.
And whatever you think, feel, believe,
and take in for processing
makes you what you are.
Because what you think, feel, believe,
and take in for processing
is the fuel that powers
the energy-to-matter-to-energy process
that results in the ongoing creation of
both your body and your spirit.

So moment by moment,
you actually and literally create yourself.
And make yourself what you are.

When you are out of affinity with this process,
you make yourself sick
and you make yourself better
seemingly at random.

You make yourself sick
by ignoring the messages
that your body sends out to you.
Illness is always a sign
that you have not paid attention
to an inner need for a change.
Or that you have not faced a problem.
Or that you have buried a feeling or emotion.
It's a physical memo from your body
encouraging you to listen to your problem,
release a repressed emotion,
and make whatever corrective adjustments
are needed
in your over-all life pattern.

You make yourself better
by just allowing your natural wellness
and ability to stay that way
to take over.
And by moving out of the fields, patterns,
and situations that require
messages like symptoms or medical problems
to point out that they're not for you.

In healing meditation explorations,
you reverse the process of making yourself sick.
And you recreate
all the inner and outer connections
that can keep you well.

Internally,
you have a vast and highly efficient network
of natural healers to work with you:
Your cells.
Each cell in your body,
in its own right,
wants to be well and is programmed
to resist and overcome illness.

Whole parts of you are newly created
every moment
through the internal workings of each cell.
And all of you is newly created
with all your cellular experiential memories
completely intact,
every seven years or less.
Given half a chance,
each cell in your body will keep itself well
by replacing or renewing itself
whenever necessary.
If you didn't get in the way of the process,
you would always be
filled with vitality and health.

Just through cellular responses
and cellular interactions
throughout each of your organs, glands,
tissues, and bones.

What gets in the way
of the way your cells work
is your beliefs about your health,
your unconsciousness of symptom messages,
and your willingness to stay sick
for whatever reasons or beliefs got you sick
in the first place.

That's hard to take.
But it's true.
And it's a fundamental source of illness
you can easily correct
by establishing an internal framework for health
based upon the willingness of
your body and your mind
to work together, cure each other, and be well.

Externally,
your supply of natural healing energy
is just as vast
as your inner network of cells.
Nature is on your side,
facilitating healing
as much as you are willing to let it.
Like when you were a child
and you cut yourself
and you could almost see the wound close.
Maybe now you think the band-aid did it.
But guess what!

You and nature
linked together with loving, nurturing care
did it.

And by reproducing
the conditions that allow that linkage,
you can heal yourself.
And even use your healing energies to help
anyone you love.
Without the drugs and sedatives
that mask your symptoms,
delay and disengage your cellular messages,
and drag out the whole process of getting better.

You can become conscious
of your natural inclination towards health,
your natural healing ability,
and your natural power
from the interaction of your spirit and flesh
each moment of your life.
Starting now.

Getting to know you

One of the first steps toward healing yourself
is knowing yourself.
This exploration will put you
in intimate contact with your body.

Lie down on your back
on a rug or comfortable mat,
and enter into
complete meditation.

Then,
imagine yourself shrinking and shrinking
until you have become a miniature person.
When you are smaller than half an inch,
decide in a general way where you would like to explore
inside your body.
And see yourself entering your own body
at the opening nearest that point.

For now, you'll just be going in
for a look around.

As you proceed,
begin a running commentary
about your trip inside
as if you were a tv news reporter
on location.
Look around and describe everything
you experience.

You might sound like this:
I am now completing my climb
to the left nostril
and crawling inside.
It is like a cave filled with stringy filaments.
It is dark and damp.
I switch on my light and continue on.
Further back,
there is a drop-off like a deep hole.
I can jump
or let myself down slowly with a rope.
It's slippery in this throat
so I'll climb down carefully on my rope.

Continue to describe your descent.
Tell what you see and what you feel
each step of the way.
If you chose a specific destination,
tell how you get there
through the tissues, muscles, organs,
or other obstacles.
If you are just looking around,
keep a running commentary on what you see.

Then describe your journey out again
when you're done.
Right up to the point
when you are outside your meditating body

and you expand or blow yourself up
to normal size
and merge with your body again.

Don't hurry.
And don't leave any steps out.
You will encounter surprises each time
you go in
so it is essential not to preplan a storyline.
Just be there
and experience all the events as they come up.

You'll need to go back many times
before you have looked over
the whole interior territory.
And each time will be different.
But once you know where everything is,
the practical applications
of this exploration will begin.

You can enter your body and proceed directly to:
A sore muscle
and massage, squeeze, or walk on it.
A headache
and hose it away.
A blockage in a vein, artery, or passageway
and hammer or pry it loose.
A lump or foreign object anywhere
and vaporize it with a laser gun or blowtorch.

Always look over a sore place carefully.
Then determine what you need to fix it.
You may find another person or creature there.
Talk to them
and find out what they're up to.
Pay close attention to whatever dialogue occurs
and whatever your commentary covers.
You will begin to know yourself
better than you have ever known yourself before.

Healing symptoms

Another way to handle the symptom of an illness
after you have entered
complete meditation
is to see whatever part of you is sick
on your inner screen
as if it were healthy, whole, and problem-free.

Just notice it there,
radiant with health and energy
and bathed in white light,
for five minutes a day.
That's all it takes.

Sometimes,
when you're really wired in,
you'll feel better and be better
immediately.
Sometimes,
it takes three or more
five-minute meditations over three days
to notice any effect.

If you have any difficulty
getting into this
or any other healing meditation,
the bathtub meditation position on page 23
will melt away all barriers.

Always remember
that five minutes is enough
and that more isn't better.
Any longer time period
borders on preoccupation
which reinforces the weakness of a weak spot
and makes it weaker.
Dwelling on a symptom is as harmful

in the long run
as running from it, ignoring it
or being unconscious of it.

Just noticing it,
focusing your energy in and around it
and seeing it well on your screen
automatically dissolves the beliefs
that produced the symptom
in the first place.
And stimulates your natural inner desire
to be well and stay well.

Symptoms,
whether you can specifically identify them
or not,
are simply indications that
something needs caring for.
Complete meditation
creates all the space you need
to care for it.

Healing pain

Sudden pain
from headache, strained muscles,
and other places that hurt,
can be sent away
just as suddenly as it came.

Shift your concentration
for a few moments
onto getting yourself into
complete meditation
or a state reasonably close to it.
Then
allow your awareness to flow back
to the area of pain.

And describe it completely to yourself
from the framework of four questions:
How big is it in inches or in feet?
What color is it?
What shape is it?
How thick is it?

As quickly as you can,
without thinking about anything else,
go back to the top of the list again.
How big is it now?
What color is it now?
What shape is it now?
How thick is it now?

Notice any changes in size or color
and again without thinking about it further,
go back to the top of the list again.
How big is it now?
What color is it now?
What shape is it now?
How thick is it now?
Notice the changes, if any.
And go back to the top of the list
again.

Keep running through the list.
Ask yourself each question.
Find the answer in the substance of the pain.
Answer to yourself.
Go on to the next question.

Within minutes,
you will notice that your pain is becoming
smaller, lighter, thinner
and gone.

Healing chronic problems

The point about any chronic problem is
that your belief that it is chronic
and your mental pictures that it is chronic
make and keep it chronic.
This explanation can break the cycle.
Enter into
complete meditation.
And direct one ray of your awareness
to the area where the problem is.
Don't do anything else for a moment or two.
Just notice the entire area.

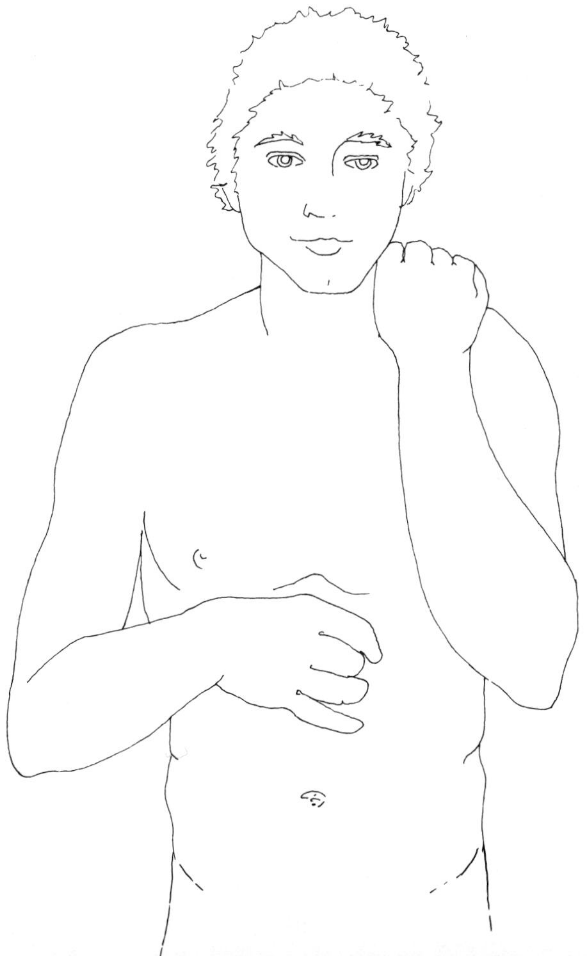

Then direct still another ray
of your awareness
to your heart, root, solar or splenic chakra.
These chakras have the most direct effect
on self-healing
so use whichever one is closest
to your problem area
or most active when you reach inside
to contact it.

Link your awareness securely to both places.
And like an inner electrician,
wire the two rays of awareness together.
When your chakra is feeding directly
into your so-called chronic problem,
allow your chakral energy
to fully enter the problem area.

At first,
it may help
to place one hand over your problem area
and the other hand over your chakra.
And allow the link to form through your hands.
To do this most effectively,
your left hand must be
in the higher position on your body
or closer to your head than your right hand.

Remain in meditation
with a clear screen
and allow the energy to flow inside of you.
Just before you're ready to
break the connection,
experience fully
the reality of your problem area.
And notice whatever emotion
and whatever beliefs, pictures, or sensations
are there.

Allow them to flow
into the connected energy screen
between your problem and your chakra.

One complete meditation
will trigger the healing process
you need.
And you may feel the effects immediately.
However, you may repeat the process
if you like.
Just don't overdo it.
Conditions that take years to form
can occasionally disappear overnight.
More often,
they require a few weeks to a few months
to totally dissolve.
And then,
as your cells
recreate and rebuild each and every part of you,
you will have made it possible
for them to recreate and rebuild
your chronic problem area
without your chronic problem in it.

Healing chronic beliefs

Any serious meditative work
from this section on
requires some long hard looks at
the beliefs or habitual mind pictures
that come up in your life
and cause you to be sick
or less powerful than you really are
in any way.

This exploration will clear you
from any healing problem
you encounter now.

And you can adapt it to cover
any negative belief
that creates an evolutionary problem
or development barrier
later on.

Choose any area of your health
that you believe to be a problem for you.
It might be your weight,
persistant pains,
migraine headaches,
a tired de-energized feeling,
catching one cold after another,
or whatever.
Then memorize the following directions
or tape them on your cassette recorder.
And run them by
on your inner screen
when you have entered complete meditation.

Directions:
For the next ten minutes
I agree to suspend my beliefs
in this one area
and I will insert instead
the belief I want.
For this one small period of time
what I desire and what I believe
will merge and become
one and the same.
And there can be no conflict about it
because I want to do it
and I willingly agree to do it.
For the next ten minutes,
even though I merely sit here silently,
I will totally change my old belief.
And in my mind,
I will accept my new belief
and my intention to act on it
as if it were fully my own.

Then,
for ten minutes,
put the words or pictures
that best describe a revised version of
your most chronic and harmful old belief
on your screen.
If you believe you are overweight,
see yourself as slender as you want to be
or see the words,
''The ideal weight for me is______pounds.''
If you believe you are not healthy,
see clearly the words, the picture,
or the belief that you are supremely healthy.

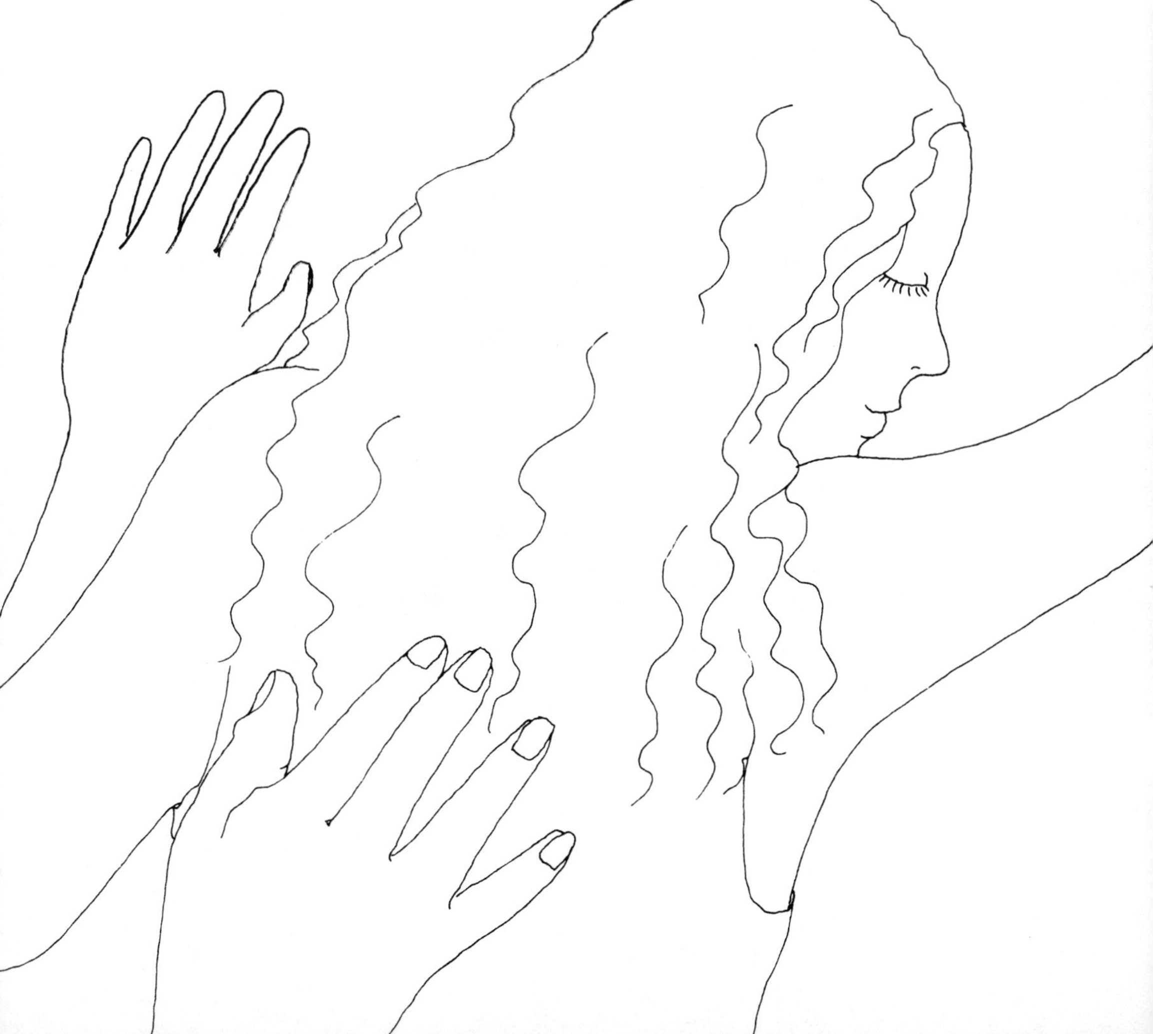

Don't change any actions
outside of your meditation.
Keep everything else exactly as it has been.
And keep your meditation
strictly to the agreed-upon ten minutes.
And then forget about it
for the rest of the day.

In less than a month,
you will begin to see
your new belief
beginning to take shape and form
in your reality and your experience.
You will notice it most directly
in the form of new impulses and desires
that will become increasingly stronger
as you act on them.

At this point,
you can begin to revise another
chronic belief
in the same manner.
And create the same type of change
in still another area of your health
or your life.

This exploration,
like all meditations of this type,
works
for reasons that defy explanation.
All of them work fastest and easiest
when you do them
without making comparisons to normal events
and without making judgements.
You don't need to understand what is happening
for it to happen.
Just as you don't need to understand
how gravity works
for gravity to work for you.

Trusting yourself
and the process of your life
is really all that is required.

Healing someone else

Knowing how to
take miniature journeys through the body,
dissolve symptoms and pains,
and apply chakral energy
will also produce miraculous results
when you apply them to someone else.

First,
be certain that you have tried the techniques
and that they work consistently for you,
just the way they are supposed to do.
Then,
be equally certain that you are working with
someone who is willing to be healed.
If you are in doubt, just ask directly.
In fact, asking and affirming
that your friend is willing to be healed
makes your role in the process
ninety percent easier.

Even when you know
you have an unlimited supply available,
you don't need to waste your energy
on anyone who wants to fight you
for the privilege of remaining unwell.

When you are ready to begin,
bring your breathing and your vibratory rate
down to a meditational level,
and try whichever of these variations
work best for you.

The miniature exploration
tends to work best
when the other person is
either lying still and breathing deeply
or somewhere else altogether.
Visualize yourself becoming tiny
and entering your friend's body,
locating the source of pain or illness,
observing it gently and lovingly
and then fixing it
with whatever seems to make sense at the time.

Keep a running commentary going,
silently if you wish,
until you have merged yourself
back into your own body.
Visualizing a symptom
bathed in energy and light
and looking healthy, revitalized and well
can be done
from a complete or semi-meditative state
at a distance or in person.

See your friend's ailing part or organ
healthy again
against a field of bright radiance
on your inner screen.
And project the energy
from the image on your screen
to the person you want to heal.
See the healing energy leave your forehead
from the region of your brow chakra,
like white-gold light from a spotlight
bathing its target in brilliance.

Healing someone with your hands
through actual touch
or from a distance up to eighteen inches
involves the application of

chakral energy
directly to a problem area.
Have the person you are healing
lie down
on his back,
placing yourself at his right side.
Or on his stomach,
placing yourself at his left side.

While breathing slowly, deeply and rhythmically,
direct your energy to your hands.

When you can feel your energy flowing
between your hands
and you become aware of heat or tingling,
hold your left hand palm down
about a foot over your friend's body.
Pass your hand over his body
from his toes to his head,
lingering lightly over each area
that you know to contain a chakra.
And feel for the same type of energy flow you get
when your own palms are facing each other.

Energy that you can sense
pulsing or radiating from a foot away
is flowing well and doing well.
Energy so weak or blocked
that you cannot feel it
unless you lower your hand,
requires attention.

Note the areas that need your help.
And when you complete your hand scan,
come back to them.
Link your right hand to
your friend's left knee chakra
or root chakra.

Hold your left hand on or over
any weak upper chakral point
and wire his energy together,
using your hands to start the flow
through the chakral circuit.
When you sense
the fluttering, radiating pulse,
the connection is complete.

When energy is flowing
throughout your friend's body
at a consistent and unblocked rate,
you can turn your awareness
to the area of reported illness.
With your left hand
always in a higher position on the body
than your right,
connect your friend's
root, splenic, solar or heart chakra
(whichever is pulsing the strongest)
to the area of pain, illness or disturbance.

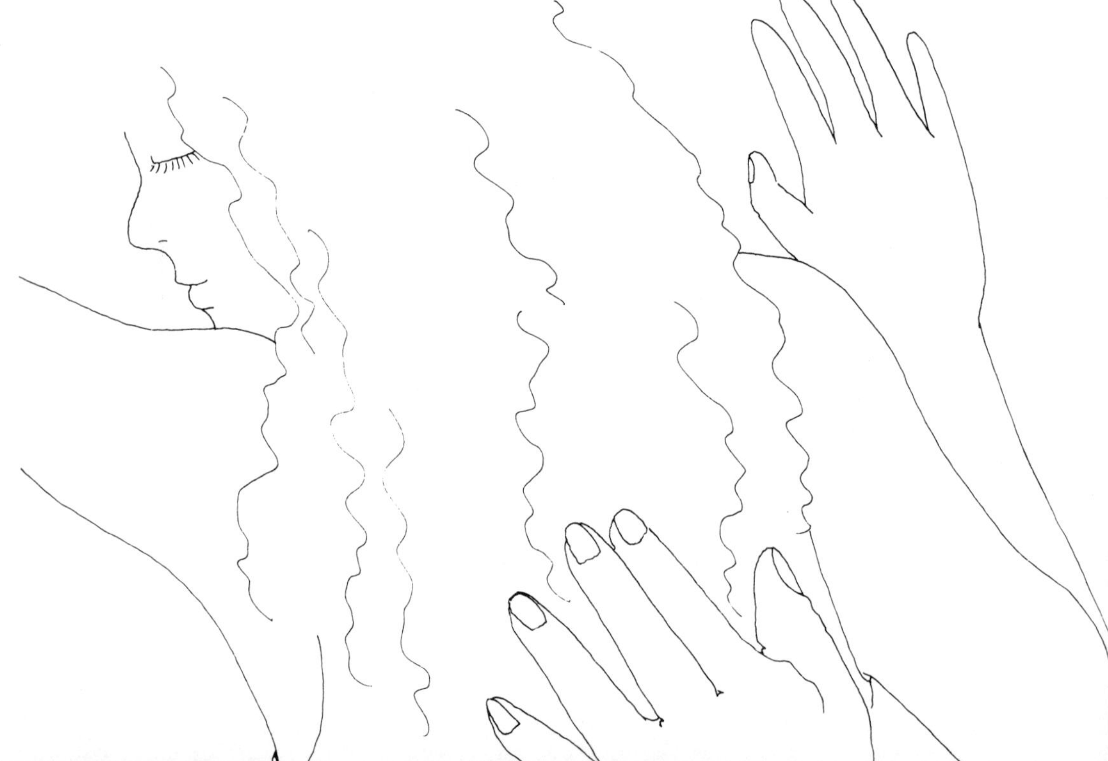

Keep your hands in place
on your friend's body
or a few inches over it
until you can feel freely flowing energy
from the chakra to the healing zone.
Then wait a minute or two longer.
And allow your own energy to reinforce
the flow of life force
just like a strong battery can be used
to power a weaker one
through connecting cables,
until the engine starts generating power
on its own.

If you like or if you feel you need to,
you can visualize
the color of the chakra you are using
or chant Ommmmm
to its appropriate musical pitch.

When you feel the healing is completed,
slowly lift your hands.
Allow them to linger over the contact points
you have established
for a few moments
before you remove them altogether.
If your hands feel at all
sticky or itchy,
shake them vigorously behind you
and rinse them in cool water.

Chakral healings like this
can produce truly unbelieveable results
in less than 30 minutes.

Strengthening your healing power

In reality,
more strength and power
than you can ever possibly use up
is already wired into your cells
and fully available
to keep you well
and to keep you engineering your life
to your own blueprints.

This exploration will
strengthen your connection
to your own source of power
and enable you to use your natural healing skill
willfully.
Whenever you wish.

Enter into complete meditation.
On your inner screen,
allow an image of the universe to form.
And see it.
Just fully see it.
Notice the infinite expanse
of countless suns and stars,
planets, comets, novas and galaxies,
all whirling and bursting and glowing
with energy enough
to light all the limitless space in between.

Become aware of the indescribable energy
that fills your universe.
And notice how
it flashes and flares and glows and radiates
in every color imaginable.

Notice too,
the sounds and vibrations
resonating

from each whirling star, planet
and galactic system that you see.
And observe how the sounds
harmonize
in a vast orchestral symphony of life.

Now allow a shape,
an outline of a human body,
to form
overlaid against the universe on your screen.
And watch the outline
as you allow it to slowly expand
to fill all the space you can see.

Watch.
As the shape of the outline body
begins to encompass
all of the bodies of energy in the universe.
Your stars and suns and moons and comets
and all the space between
have not become smaller.
But the outline shape
of the human body
has grown large enough to take them all in.

Observe.
As the body fills with light,
the outline glows with an inner radiance
that flares outward
in rays extending far beyond the outlined body.
When it is almost too bright to watch anymore,
the rays subside.
And features appear in the outline.

The features are your own.

Simultaneously,
the body that fills your screen
shifts position

and merges into your own body.
Until you and your image are one and the same.

As you re-enter your space
from complete meditation,
your source of power and cellular energy
has become clear to you.
It is now available to you
on a conscious level
to keep you well
and enable you to attain your goals.

Dynamic meditation

Dynamic meditation

Being able to create change and transformation
in your life
is the most dynamic use
of applied energy in
complete meditation.
It is also the most subtle.
Because you can't change something that is
by hoping,
by trying to
or by chipping away at it
little by little.

All that does is cause it to persist.
To create change
you must create transformation
literally from nothing
to whatever it is that you want.

The subtle part involves
allowing whatever you want to change
to stay the way it is,
knowing that you created it the way it is,
and then
moving on
to whatever comes next.

For instance,
if you are lonely,
you can't change it
by complaining,
by wishing for your true love to appear,
or by forcing yourself
into tense and uncomfortable social situations.

You can transform it
by noticing how lonely you really are
and fully experiencing

all the sensations and feelings
of your loneliness,
by realizing that you created your loneliness
and that you are the sole cause of it,
and by moving on
to a state of non-loneliness
in which your loneliness dissolves away
all by itself.

The dynamic part involves
knowing that you can bring
everything you want into your life
whenever you want it.
And then doing exactly that.
Consciously and by intent.
Instead of allowing
unconscious belief systems and premises
filled with conflict and contradictions
to control the exchange and flow
between you and the universe.

For example:

If part of you believes
it's great to be rich
and part of you believes
it's selfish to be rich,
you'll probably never have a lot of money.

If part of you believes
cancer runs in your family,
you'll probably never live to see 85.

If part of you believes
you are not wonderful and lovable,
you'll probably spend a lot of time
alone and unhappy.

And if part of you believes
the world is filled with
crooks and conmen and troublemakers,
guess who you'll keep running into
again and again?

But the idea is not
to change the beliefs that you are
selfish, disease-prone, unworthy of love
or headed for a disaster-filled encounter.
The idea is
to notice that you may believe
things like that to be true.
And that your beliefs
may be creating things like that
in your environment and your life
just to support and perpetuate themselves.
Then let all of that be
the way it is.
And move along to something else
that you really want to be, do or have
instead.

That's the way transformation works.
And these next explorations
will get it working for you.

Warming up

Settle into
your most comfortable meditation position
and breathing pattern.
When you have entered complete meditation,
hold your hands
a comfortable distance apart
with your palms facing each other.
Let your fingers relax.

Slowly bring your hands closer and closer
until you begin to feel
the energy field between them.
If you've never done it before,
the sensation will seem like
what happens when you try to bring
the southern poles of two magnets
together.

Will the energy to flow
between your hands.
And support your will
by keeping your breath deep, low and intense,
until you become aware of heat or tingling.

As the energy field becomes more powerful,
begin to program it.

Start by projecting
a clearly formed picture
of a tangible object or concept you want to have.
Beam it from your inner screen
directly into the center of your energy field.
Actually see what you want
between your hands
right in the middle of all the energy and power
you've created.
And hold it there.
Allow your breath
to fan the fire and warmth,
as you allow a steady stream of love
to flow into the field
from your heart chakra.

Continue to hold what you want
between your hands
until you feel it begin to
take on a life of its own.
At that moment,
you'll sense a feeling of completion.

So release your thought object or idea
with love.
It will go into the physical world
and gather all the physical matter it needs
to become real.

Giving form to your thoughts,
or creating thought-forms,
as this process is called,
is the simplest and most direct way
to materialize your wants.

Releasing old beliefs

Rest assured
that the one area of your life
you want to change the most
is the one area of your life
in which your beliefs
are in strongest conflict.

Isolate that area now.
And enter into
complete meditation.

Visualize
that your body
has turned to clear transparent glass.
And take a moment to get used
to how it feels to have a clear glass body.
Notice all the stuff in it
and all the debris that you've accumulated.

Now visualize that a soapy bubbly fluid
is beginning to pour into your glass body
through the top of your head.
As you watch,

the fluid fills your body
from your toes up to your head
and sloshes around
like the soapy water in a washing machine.

Notice how the fluid turns a rusty color
as it scrubs and cleanses
the sum total of your inner beliefs
in the area that you've chosen to open up
for change.

Experience the sensations
of the rusty sudsy fluid
of your outmoded beliefs
splashing into each hidden corner
of your glass body
with a steady, pulsing, agitated rhythm.

Now,
notice that each of your fingertips
has a valve you can open.
Open each valve
and watch the rusty fluid
flow out,
leaving your head, neck, shoulders,
arms and hands
clean and clear and sparkling.

When the last drops have drained
out of your fingers,
notice that each of your toes
also has a valve that you can open.
Open your toe valves
and watch
as the rest of your rusty belief fluid
slowly drains away.

Become aware
that nothing clings or sticks
to the inner surfaces
of your transparent glass body.
And that your breath now flows freely
through you.
Without binding and without pressure.

Close the valves in your fingers and toes.
And leave your meditation
completely unobstructed and clear
in the area you chose to transform.
All of your beliefs in that area of your life
will have drained away.
And you can start again,
fresh, bright, and clean,
with only your moment-to-moment experience
to guide you.
And help you bring in what you want.

A place to work

Many people love
the formlessness and freedom of
complete meditation,
not needing a permanent structure or place to be
in their alpha level
to be creative and productive.

Many other people love structure more.
And resist meditation
because it seems too mental or groundless.
If you're one of these people,
this exploration will give you
a permanent base
where you can go
to work, study, create, think, relax,

play and build
whenever you're in alpha.
And also see and do
everything there is to see and do
in the universe.

Even if you're not into form and structure,
a place of your own like this
might be just what you need
to get away from stress
or to visit on vacations.

Sit in a comfortable position.
And plan on remaining in it
for at least 45 minutes.

Allow your breath to flow
deeply and rhythmically
in and out of your body.
When all is still and your inner screen is clear,
start scanning for the location
where your place will be.
You can have it anywhere you want it.
On the beach. On a mountain top.
In a tree. In the middle of a pine forest.
In a hill like a hobbit.
Or at the top of a skyscraper.

Choose your location now.
And begin looking around to see
whatever is there.
Notice the terrain,
the landscape to the right and left of you,
any natural or man-made objects
in your environment,
any other people, animals or lifeforms.

Then,
begin to visualize
the size and shape of your place.

And after that,
create a stockpile of all the materials
you need to build it.
Put your place together according to
your inner plans.

Building is easier when you are in
complete meditation.
Metal framework can quickly be bent to shape.
Wood cuts effortlessly.
Glass forms itself to your design.
And stones and bricks
practically cement themselves in place.

Complete the exterior.
Put on a door
and a doorlock if you need one.
Don't forget your windows.
Then try the door. And go inside.

Visualize the finish you want
on your interior walls.
And finish them off.
if you're getting tired,
bring in as many workmen as you like
to help you.
Next, take care of the floor.
Visualize the kind of flooring you want.
And the kind of floor covering too.
And put it all in.

Then lie down on your floor
and look at the entire expanse of your place.
Experience all the feelings you get
from simply being there.

After a little while,
you can begin to furnish your place
with whatever you need or want to have there.
Since your place has access
to any point in space or time,
you can literally have anything
from anywhere or anywhen.

Like:

A telephone.
On which you can talk to anyone
who ever lived or who ever will live.

A file.
With access to all the information there is
on any person or any event
that ever was, is or will be.
All arranged alphabetically and chronologically.

A digital clock.
One that you can preset
backwards or forwards
to any time, day or year.

Hook it up to a built-in video screen
so you'll be able to see and hear
what's going on whenever you set your clock.

A transporter beam.
With which you can instantly materialize
anyone you want to see in your place.
Anytime you want to see them.

A closet.
Where you can keep everything you need.
Including all the
skills and talents and knowledge you have
but don't use.
Whenever you want,
you can take any of it out
and try it on or use it
to further develop it.

If there's anything else you want in your place,
put that in now.
You might need a desk or workbench
and a few comfortable chairs.
You are limited only by your imagination
whenever you are in your place.
And as you may be beginning to realize,
that's unlimited.

Try out everything in your place
at least once,
and get to know how it works.
If you have any questions about anything there,
just look up the answer in your file.
Or call someone who knows on your telephone.
Or transport your guides in for a meeting.

When you finally leave,
know that you have created your place,
that it is good,

and that you can return there
whenever you wish
to make anything happen in your life
that you want to have happening in your life.
From now on,
with a place like yours,
that's going to be easier and easier to do
than ever before.

Materializing your wants

Love, money, success and abundance
are all fundamental wants
that you are already empowered to bring
into your life and keep there.
What you need to know is
whatever is keeping you from these wants
is also something you have brought
into your life and are keeping there:
Your own conflicting or negative beliefs.

Consider
for a moment
how really successful and evolved creatures
like babies and small animals
get what they want.

When your little baby is
hungry or wet or lonely,
he wants to be fed or changed or held.
As he cries out his wants,
he is expressing his intention to be cared for
and the certainty that
by putting his energy into the problem,
he will solve it.

When your little kitten is stalking a bird,

his complete concentration and intent
are focused on his goal.
Every cell and sensory system in his body
are tuned in to that one objective.
And there is no confusion
about the rightness or wrongness of the issue.
He knows that cats and birds
have been in agreement about this hunting game
for millions of years.
And that both are playing to win.

Notice that whenever the bird wins,
your kitten immediately goes on
to something else
without questioning his worth as a cat
or his capacity for success.
He knows that there is as much fun
in the game
as in the victory.

You can figure out
the parallels in your own life
for yourself.
In this exploration.

Enter into
complete meditation
with one concrete thing that you want
clearly on your mind.
Concrete means
don't just think of love,
think of one specific person
whose love you want to materialize.
Don't just think of money,
think of the one specific thing
you want to buy
with all the extra money
you want to create for yourself.

Let nothing come between you and your want
for five full minutes.
Feel with certainty
that the full intensity of your emotions,
your thoughts, and your psyche
are fully focused on your one want.
And feel that you already have it.
Visualize what you want on your inner screen
and see yourself enjoying it.
Use words, if you like,
to describe your pleasure with it.

Then,
after five minutes,
forget about this meditation completely.
And go on to whatever comes up next.

Later in the day,
reinforce your meditation
by performing one simple physical gesture
just as you would do it
if you already had what you want to have.

If what you want is love,
for just one moment,
smile at someone.
Or walk into a room
looking just as alive and aglow as you would
if you had the lover you wanted.

If what you want is money,
buy yourself an extra magazine or treat.
Or get the shirt that costs five dollars more,
the next time you're out shopping.
Just as if you had the money you wanted.

By choosing one specific want
in one specific area of your life
at one time,
seeing yourself having it
in complete meditation,
acting for a moment in reality
as if you do indeed have it,
and giving up your preoccupation
with whatever went wrong in the past,
you will soon see
how you can begin to have
exactly what you want.

Chants, affirmations, incantations

Chants, affirmations and incantations
are like mantras
when you use them in meditation.

Chants are repeated aloud over and over
as rhythmically as possible.
Affirmations and incantations
are also spoken aloud
and may or may not be repeated,
although repetition reinforces them.

Especially when you're first beginning
to use them.

The places to use
chants, affirmations and incantations
are in complete meditation.
And in the crossing-over territory
between waking and sleeping.
And any other time you want to.

Just as mantras
can get you into
complete meditation,
chants, affirmations and incantations
can get you into affinity
with your power to create transformation
in your own life.

Chants include
all the mantras you may already know
that carry energy for change.
Like:
Om. For more harmony with the universe.
Shanti. For more inner peace.
She loves me. For more acceptance from
someone else.

Chants also include
short rhymes or rhythmic phrases
you can make up yourself.
Like:
More money now. More money now.
And:
No more worry, no more fear;
Now the job I want is here.

Affirmations cover
all kinds of positive things
you want to have happen
in a sort of broad and abstract way.

Like:
Every day I am getting more and more loveable.
And:
I have a lot to offer and everyone appreciates it.
And:
I am (insert your name) and I am enough.

Affirmations can also be longer
and rhythmic.
Such as:
I will give love and receive it;
I will take love and not leave it;
I'll enjoy love and not grieve it;
I will find love and believe it.

Incantations usually have
more emotional power and more intent
behind them
than either chants or affirmations.
They are like the spells
of old-time wizards and sorcerers.
And they are
very specific and very fast to work
because they acknowledge
the force of your own will.

A particularly powerful incantation
to protect you from other people's
negativity or unpleasantness
goes like this.
Visualize yourself bathed in white light,
completely surrounded by mirrored armor.
And say:
Evil bounce to he or she
who wishes that it come to me;
As I will, so mote it be
fully automatically.
An incantation to improve
your over-all environmental space
can be:

Now my psyche creates for me
abundance, work, and more money,
lots more health and energy;
As I will, so mote it be.

Once you get the idea,
you can follow the form and create
your own incantations
to cover any conceivable situation.
The word "mote" is a more positive form of
the word "might."
It also serves to hook your incantation into
the ancient forces and power
associated with incantations
since the dawn of the Age of Taurus,
sixty-four centuries ago.

Because they are highly charged statements
of what you want
and because they are empowered by
the sound of your voice,
unless your own contradictory beliefs get in the way,
the energy of
the chants, affirmations and incantations
that you put forth
always return to you
with whatever you wanted
attached to it.

Sexual power

For untold eons,
primitive cultures
and many not-so-primitive cultures alike
have known about and applied
the latent natural power
of the sexual chakra.

Early worshipers of phallic and vaginal gods,
alchemists, witches and kundalini yogis
are all in agreement about
the force of sexuality
and how to apply it to get what you want
to happen in your life.
And the basic idea about how it works
has never changed.
To create changes or materialize a want,
you dam up your sexual energy,
allow it to grow and build in intensity
and then let it explode
where you choose to focus it:
In a ritual, an incantation
or a two-person version of
complete meditation.

It works
for the same reason
that salmon battle their way upstream
to reproduce,
that migratory birds and animals migrate
and that male dogs travel for miles and miles
to court your female dog
when she comes in heat.
Sex has a mystical power all its own.

To control this power,
many religions and philosophies
advocate celibacy.
Their theory is that
abstaining and avoiding sexual thoughts and activities
raises your sexual energy
to a higher chakra
where it can be expressed
emotionally or mentally
in higher spiritual activities.
They're only part right.

To release your sexual energy
in a superintense and focused way,
you need to abstain from sex
for a specific period of time,
usually a few days to a week.
But during that time,
you need to fan the flame
of the sexuality you are damming up
by thinking and acting
as provocatively as you can.

Begin by choosing a partner to work with you.
Explain your intentions
and ask for
complete cooperation and support.
Then set aside a specific time
three to seven days in advance
when you will focus your sexual energy
together,
to create what you want in your life.
Use each day
as a period of foreplay and excitation.
And encourage your sexual energy to build
to the point of explosion.

Specifically:
Flirt with each other.
Touch and pet and tease each other.
Wear whatever fantasy clothing turns you on.
Read sexually explicit magazines and novels.
Go to X-rated movies.
Excite and arouse each other shamelessly.
And come as close as you can
to the act of sex itself
without ever crossing that line
or experiencing an orgasm.

During this period of
waiting and arousal,
allow your sexual energy to rise each day
to a higher chakra
in a complete meditation
where you focus
on a daily chant, affirmation or incantation
that graphically describes
whatever you want to transform
in your life.

Finally,
when the time to end the waiting arrives,
join your partner.
And go to your bedroom or your meditation space
together.
Light candles and incense
and keep the setting romantic and erotic.
Remove each other's clothing
and body jewelery.
And lightly stroke and caress
each other's genitals, abdomen, solar plexus,
chest, throat, and brow
as you chant your incantation
over and over.

When you are ready,
lie down together
and as you continue to touch and caress,
visualize the thought or object you want
in the space just above you both,
much as you did
when you created thought-forms
in the exploration on pages 185 and 187.

Energize your visualization together
as your excitation builds and builds.
And you begin to make love.

When you are ready,
join together
and allow your orgasmic energy
to encompass your visualization.
At the point of explosion,
affirm as loudly as you both can:
"It is beginning now!"

After you scream out the words,
let all of your remaining energies
merge into your visualization.
And as you quietly lie together,
stroking each other,
gently and lovingly
send your thought-form on its way.

It will soon return to your life
in totally materialized form.

Sexual energy
is the ultimate source of empowerment
for dynamic change and transformation.
You won't need to use it very much.
And for smaller wants,
it tends to have the same effect
as dropping a bomb on an ant hill.

But whenever you have
a major miracle to materialize
or a really burning want,
you now have the power source
that can bring it in.
It's the same power source you always had.
Only now,
you know how to fuse it and use it.

Psychic meditation

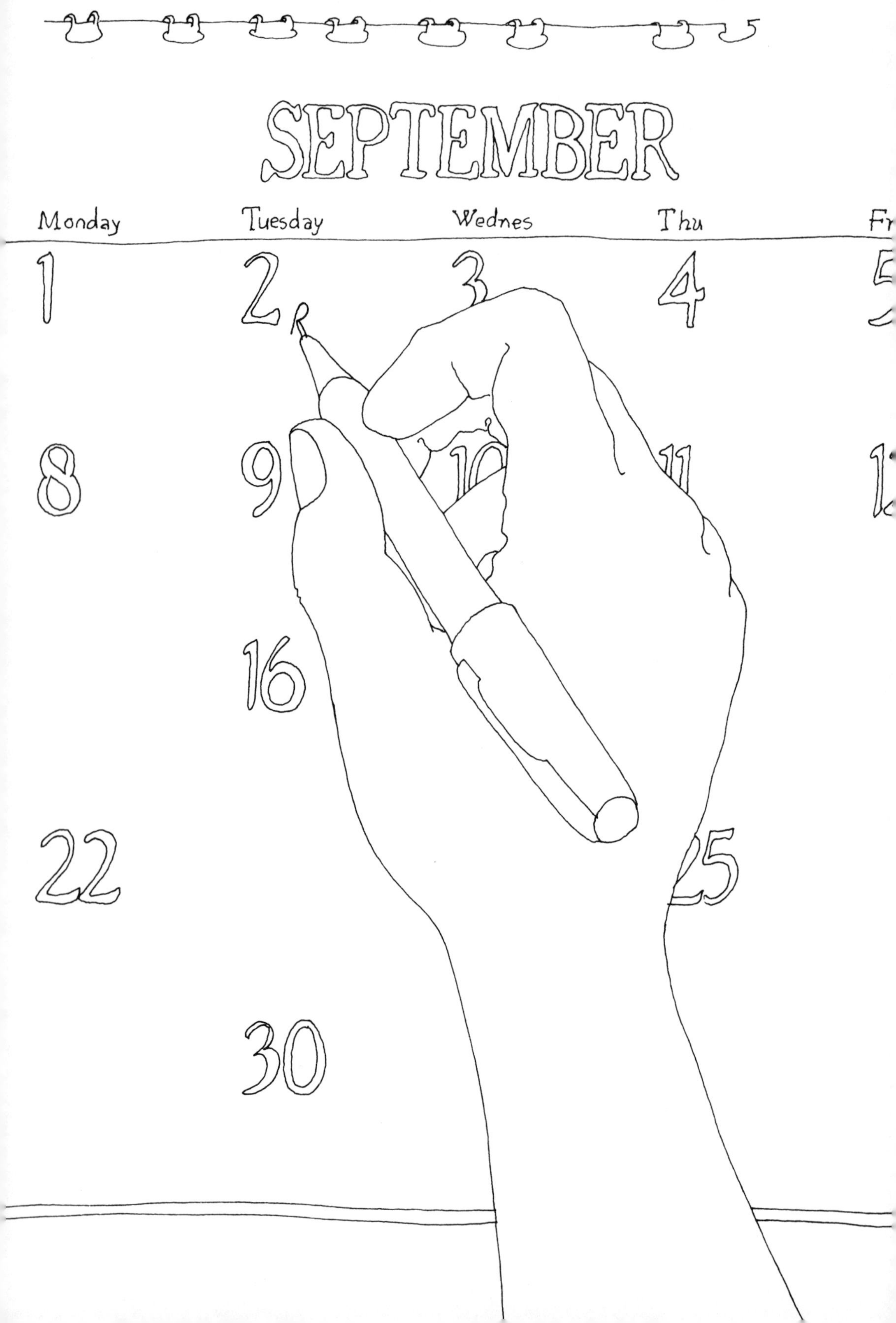

SEPTEMBER

Monday Tuesday Wednes Thu Fr

1 2 3 4 5

8 9 10 11 1

16

22 25

30

Psychic meditation

Being psychic
is not limited to only a few
so-called psychics.
Being psychic
is a part of simply being.
And the only reason
why you can't communicate telepathically,
really grok other people and know them,
or foretell what's coming up next,
is that you closed off
those and other similar avenues of expression
long ago.

Everyone is born with psychic ability.
You notice it most strongly
in early childhood
before you buy the lie that it's not so.

In early childhood,
you accepted all of your emerging powers
as a living creature
without questioning or evaluating them.
You discovered with wonder and delight
that you could walk and talk
and hold a spoon and control your body functions
and read a book.
You also discovered with wonder and delight
that you could see other creatures
in the space around you,
and enjoy lots of invisible friends and playmates,
and talk to trees and rays of sun,
and know when Uncle Morris was coming
with a present,
and sense all the other families of beings
you shared past, present and future lives with.

But because you were acknowledged
for the first group of powers
and not the second,
you let your psychicness lie
fallow and unexplored.
And you became a product of your culture.

Incredible as it may seem,
there are still places in the world today
where knowing
how to manipulate material objects around you
with your mind,
and communicate with thoughts
instead of words,
are more praised and acclaimed
attributes of humanity
than knowing
how to choose a jacket that matches
your slacks.

The happy ending is that
your psychic gifts have not left you,
even though you may think
you've left them behind.
Still waiting in unopened gift boxes
deep in the closets of your subconscious,
you can find them,
develop them,
and play with them
as you were meant to.
In complete meditation.

The basic approach is
to clear your mind and your screen
with the intention
that an image or sound will appear there,
relating to what you want to know or do
in the world around you.

The images or sounds you receive
may be absolutely literal data
or strange symbols that require translation
before they can be understood
and applied.

The point,
in either case,
is that what you get is what you got,
that it is accurate and correct
with no other considerations or evaluations,
and that there is a message in it for you
telling you
something you need or want to know.

This is the principle
that allows
all your psychicness
to more fully emerge and flourish.

Whenever you begin to doubt
the power of your inner images,
it retreats.
Just as it did so many years ago
when you were very young
and you bought the lie that
your psychic ability was unreal,
impractical,
or just plain nonsense.

Whenever you begin to accept
the power of your inner images
to transcend the barriers of space and time,
it grows.
Just as it is meant to grow
in order to become
a more and more enriching and stabilizing force
in your life.

This, once again, is The Force.
It's the only force you've got.
And you'll know why you feel
a tingle of recognition
each time you see it in the Star Wars sagas,
when you see that
it may indeed be with you.

In these explorations,
you'll find it useful
to keep a small notebook near you.
So you can write down
the date and time of your meditation,
and the images, impressions and messages
that you pick up.

Psychometry

Psychometry is the ability
to read the history or perceive a story
about a piece of jewelry
or other small object
by simply touching it
and tuning into its vibrations
or the memories of its cells.

All cells live
because all cells are in motion in time,
existing with a purpose
from way back there
to somewhere else up ahead.
All living cells possess memories
filled with data even more accurate
than computer chips and semiconductor wafers.
And the vibrations from cellular memories
include visual and other sensory data
that can tell you the complete story.

Start by selecting any object
or piece of jewelry
that you don't ordinarily wear or carry
all the time.
Something you've just bought
or a friend's possession
is ideal for this exploration.

Enter complete meditation
with the object in your hand.
And allow its story to unfold on your screen.

Don't do anything.
Just hold the object gently in your hand.
Press it to your abdomen, your diaphragm,
or your brow chakra if you like.
And be receptive to whatever happens next.

You may see a previous owner
or a string of previous owners.
You may see your friend
in a situation that has passed
or one that will come to pass.
You may catch glimpses of
other eras, other times, other cultures.
You may even hear a name
or a narrative like a radio story.

By not trying to do anything
and not reaching for anything,
you allow it all to happen to you.
All by itself.

Telepathy

Thought transference is what
telepathy is all about.
There are two sides to the process.
Sending your thoughts to someone else.
And receiving thoughts from someone else.
There is no question that
you can relearn how to do both,
although one or the other will seem easier
to you at first.
Telepathy is
as natural and fundamental a process
as thinking.
And if you never exercised
your mental muscles
for addition and subtraction,
you'd find them a lot harder to do
than telepathy.
Because working with numbers
is something you have to learn,
and telepathy is something you already know.

The thing about telepathy
is that conscious concentration
inhibits it.
Especially at first.
So you need to become passive
and receptive about it.
Even when you are actively engaged
in doing it.

To send your thoughts:

Enter into complete meditation
with your breathing deep and rhythmic
and your inner screen clear.
Then,
visualize the person you want to contact
on your inner screen.

Think only of the person.
Not the message.
See his face clearly.
Hear the sound of his voice.
Smell whatever scent you associate with him.
Imagine how the surface of his skin
feels to the touch.
And, if you are closely involved,
taste the taste that reminds you most of him.

Create a picture of the person
using as many of your senses as you can.
And hold that image
without doing anything else
for as long as you comfortably can.

If you are into testing and want to see results,
just before
you let your multisensory picture go,
scream out with your mind

as loudly as your mind can scream:
Call Me.
And let the image fade away.

To receive thoughts:

Enter complete meditation
and repeat
the first part of the sending process,
creating a multisensory image
of the person you want to tap into.
Use your inner ear, nose, tongue and fingers
as well as your inner eye.

Again,
hold the picture as long as you can,
without doing anything.
Keep the rest of your mind
perfectly open, clear, and receptive.

Just before you let the picture go,
downshift
all the openness, clarity and receptiveness
of your mind,
accelerating it
and at the same time
creating a powerful vacuum within yourself.

Take whatever comes first
as the message you wanted to receive.
That's it.

If you don't understand it,
write it down
and look at it a few times during the day.
Think of it as you slip into alpha
before sleep arrives that night.
Telepathy is not, at first, always precise.
But it always does come through
if you are open to it.

Later on,
you can do advanced thought transference work.
Team up with a partner.
And arrange to meditate at the same time,
no matter how far away from each other
you may be.
Practice sending each other a word.
Or a visual image like a square, star,
crescent, cloud, tree or bird.
Then go on to personal messages.

After a while,
you will find that you both can
activate that particular channel of your minds
and send and receive thoughts
anytime you want to.
Even when you are not in
complete meditation.

This exploration will give you
all the foundation you need to do it.
Practice it at different times
of the day and evening.
And use multisensory images
of many different people.
Your psychic muscles will strengthen
before you know it.

Precognition, clairvoyance, postcognition

Precognition is the ability
to see a future event
or respond to a feeling about it.
Like changing lanes on the highway
just before the car in front of you
has a blowout.
And not taking the 10:45 flight to Chicago
at the last minute
and later reading that it crashed.

Clairvoyance is the ability
to see something in the present
or near present
somewhere other than where you are.
Like knowing that an unexpected check
is on its way to you
to prevent an overdraft.
Or sensing that
a far-away friend or relative
is very ill or about to die.

Postcognition is the ability
to see a past event
that you have not personally experienced.
Like a vivid scene
from your father's childhood.
Or a clear impression of
some recent happening
in a friend's or neighbor's life.

All three of these psychic abilities
are essentially the same.
Because all of time flows
in a continuous stream
through the moment you are living in
right now,
all events are literally occurring
simultaneously.

This means
you can tune in to any event
anywhere along the stream of time
by simply widening your context,
your vantage point, and your perceptiveness
to include all the sensory impressions
that are always entering your mind.
But that you usually ignore or discount.

Moving through time
in complete meditation
is like moving through a vast field of wheat.
The wheat is all around you,
in thickly planted eight-foot stalks
waving and undulating with the breeze.

All the stalks in front of you
are yet to come.
All the stalks behind you
have aleady been passed through.
All the stalks to the right and left of you
are other moments unfolding in the present.
And the entire field of wheat
is all growing
now.

What you want to do to see
precognitively, clairvoyantly, or postcognitively
is
raise your point of sight
above the tops of the wheat stalks
and just take a look around.

You can begin to finetune this process
by really becoming aware
of all the off-the-wall impressions
that come to you
all the time.
Notice when you get a feeling
to step on your brake
before you see a dog run in front of your car.
Stop sending away or invalidating
the pictures you get glimpses of
in your head.
Give them time to develop and expand
and fill in
to become complete scenes.
Then jot down each impression you receive
after it has run its course.

Later,
when you are in
complete meditation,
visualize one of your fleeting impressions.
Recreate it on your inner screen.
Follow it, play with it.
And see where it takes you.

As you practice
catching, holding, and anchoring
your impressions,
and then pursuing them further and further
into complete meditation,
they'll take you as far as you can go.

Prediction

Using the same idea of time
that you've just explored,
you can now begin to make predictions
with a higher and higher degree
of accuracy.

Enter into
complete meditation
with a pad of paper by your side
and today's date and the word "Predictions"
at the top of a blank page.

Meditate with no specific purpose or intent
for as long as you like.
Just as you are leaving your meditative state,
write "1"
and fill in the first thing
that comes into your mind.
It doesn't matter what it is yet,
so don't think about it or evaluate it.
Just write it down.
Then write "2"
and write down the next thing
that comes into your mind.
Continue
until you have
at least three to six predictions filled in.

During the days and weeks that follow,
check your lists against
the people, objects, and events
in your life.
And cross-check your prediction lists
with any other psychic development
or dream notes you may also be keeping.

Many predictions will be right on the money.
Others will be symbols of things to come,
like the image of a child
hiding in a playground
and an unexpected visitor from Hyde Park.
Some may never come to pass at all
in this reality.
And that doesn't make you wrong.
It means you are receiving
impressions of people or events
that are surely interacting
to the right or left of you,
in the timeless wheat fields
of each moment you pass through.

As you work on predictions,
they'll become easier and easier
and much more spontaneous.
You'll probably begin to get
non-meditative glimpses and flashes
about all kinds of things to come.
Including those incredibly lucid warnings
about accidents that you can avoid.

So write down anything and everything
at first,
no matter how sketchy or foolish it may seem.
And give the connection
between your psychic awareness and conscious awareness
all the room and care it needs
to develop and grow
for you.

Psychokinesis

Whenever you are ready
to test your inner power

to create, transform or directly influence
external reality,
this exploration is the place to begin.

For the next few days,
when you enter complete meditation
project the brilliant fire of your energy
upon your screen.

Let your energy build from your lowest chakra,
deep at the base of your spine.
And let it rise upward through your spinal column
like a fire in an elevator shaft
to your brow chakra
just behind your inner screen.
Experience the heat and the power
you can create at will
in complete meditation.

And then test it.

Sit outside or at your window
on a day
when groups of fluffy white and grey clouds
are meandering across the sky.
Choose a cloud
that is neither smaller or larger
than the clouds near it.
Stare at it with a fixed gaze
through your external eyes
and project a beam of energy
through the inner eye of your brow chakra.

Watch
as your energy steadily shrinks the cloud
and causes it to disappear.
Notice that the smaller and larger clouds
all around it
are essentially unchanged.

Depending upon the force of
your energy and your intent,
the whole vaporization process
may take a few seconds.
Or a few minutes.
But no cloud can handle
the heat of your inner power.
So zap as many clouds as you like
until you get the idea that
there's nothing to it.

Then turn your attention
to more solid things.

Set a compass in front of you
on a table.
Direct your energy at it
through your brow chakral eye.
And cause the needle to swing away from north.
If you want,
point your fingers at the needle
from a distance,
and notice how you can energize the compass
with the energy in your hands.

After that,
try suspending a small object
from a thin thread
taped to the top of the inside
of a large glass or bell jar.
When you invert the container,
your object will hang down.
Direct your energy at it
through your third eye chakra
or through your hands
until it begins to move.
It will.

Finally,
hold a key or a spoon handle
lightly between your thumb and first finger.
Do not press or apply pressure.
Imagine that your energy and heat
are flowing into the metal object
and that it is beginning to bend.
You may massage the object lightly
with your thumb and finger
to stimulate your energy flow.

Watch what happens
when you don't try to make anything happen.
Children who have seen
metal-bending demonstrated on television
can sometimes duplicate the process
with no instruction at all.
So let the child in you play with this one.
And give the child permission to succeed.

Projecting your consciousness

Choose any cellular object or being
like a stone, a plant, a tree, an animal,
a person, or any inanimate possession.
If you have difficulty selecting one,
you may select as many as you like,
one at a time.

Then enter your meditative state
with the object or being somewhere near you.

When you are clear
and breathing deeply and rhythmically,
allow your energy and your consciousness
to flow into the object or being
that you selected.
Flow gently in,
wishing the object or being well.
And ask for permission to enter
if you encounter any resistance.
Then begin to let yourself
experience reality
from that point of view.
Sense the impressions you get.
See the inner and outer pictures.
And feel what life feels like
from another vantage point in the universe.

If you've chosen a tree,
for example,
notice how the roots probe so deeply
for stabilization and nourishment,
and how, in this life form,
you see the passing seasons
and sense other life forms in your environment.
Including yourself.

If you've chosen a road or a brook,
notice how you cut and wander
through physical space.
And notice all the pictures and impressions
you take in
from all the points along the path
of your being.

You can test the power of this exploration
by abruptly staring at
and focusing your consciousness on
your dog, a wild bird, a turtle or a fly.
Or even the back of someone's head
in a movie theater or on a bus.
Creatures will notice your energy
penetrating their field
before people do.
But everyone and everything will react,
look at you to see what you want,
and then withdraw, come closer
or tighten their shields.

In complete meditation
or any state close to it,
you enter other fields of energy
less abruptly and less threateningly.
So you encounter less resistance
and you can stay longer.

Projecting your consciousness
is a fascinating way
to take up the time and space
when you are waiting for a person
or an idea to arrive.
After you can do it easily in meditation,
you can simulate it anytime and anywhere
to broaden your outlook
and see reality as others see it.

Trance states

In a classic sense,
complete meditation is a trance state.
And all the preliminary definitions
and sensations of meditation
apply to trances as well.
For instance,
when you are in a trance,
you are especially apt to notice
that instead of darkness
behind your closed eyes,
there is light.
Sometimes almost blindingly intense light.

You can check your trance state
in complete meditation
by suggesting to yourself that
you cannot open your eyes.
And the harder you try,
the more tightly closed they'll remain.
You actually won't be able to open your eyes
until you release the suggestion.

You can also suggest that
when you extend an arm or leg,
it will become so rigid and stiff
that you cannot bend it.

And you won't be able to bend it,
no matter how hard you try,
until you cancel your suggestion
to yourself.

Once you know you are in
that kind of trance,
you can open your mind
to any entity you want to allow in.

Your own guides become available on the spot.
Famous artists, thinkers, and inventors
of the past and the future
can be called on to support your efforts
to solve a problem in their
areas of expertise.
Friends or relatives who have passed on
can be contacted
and all types of unfinished business
can be laid to rest.

The most concrete and literal answers
to your most pressing questions and problems
can be summoned.
Including specific solutions to health problems
and on-target career or romantic advice.

Practice trance states
at home
or wherever you are not likely
to be disturbed.
You may feel more spacey
when you emerge from a trance
than when you come out of meditation.
So allow adequate recovery time
to avoid questions and concerns of
fellow workers or casual acquaintances.

Adeptness with your trance states
can take you all the way into
full-time mediumship.
Whatever you want to do
is open to you,
when you start to do it
in the expansiveness of
complete meditation.

Astral meditation

Astral meditation

The farther you go into
complete meditation,
the more difficult it becomes to draw
tight definitional lines
around the different areas you explore.
Tight lines and rigid definitions
just don't hold up
in flowing meditative landscapes.

Astral meditation
is something like some of the explorations
you've already done
involving projecting your consciousness.
And yet,
it is so unique and so far-reaching
that, at the same time,
it's altogether something else.

In an astral meditation
or any spontaneous astral experience,
you project more than your consciousness or mind.
You actually project
your spirit, soul or energy essence
out of your body,
leaving only enough behind
to keep your body functioning and warm and safe.

It is not anywhere near as big a deal
or as traumatic an event as it sounds.
And the reason it's not
is that you have done it before.
In fact, you've had hundreds or thousands of
out-of-body experiences
since you were born.
You just never hung a label on them before.
Or consciously attempted to remember them.

If,
when you are dreaming,
everything seems particularly vivid and alive,
you have projected astrally in your sleep.
If,
when you are meditating,
you experience a humming sound,
a sensation like a large rubber band snapping,
or a peculiar heightening
of your inner vibrational state,
you are projecting astrally
right then and there.

The good thing about astral projection is
time and space have no meaning,
so you can be anywhere or anywhen
instantaneously.
You can even enter the body
of another person or a pet,
in a deeper, more profound way than you've yet done,
and see what makes them what they are.
This can be a valuable healing technique
because you can see exactly what's wrong
and fix it right there
with less of an energy expenditure
than even the little tiny person exploration.

The bad thing about astral projection is
its press.
It is a misunderstood phenomenon.
And a lot of unnecessary
fear, warning and cautions
have been rattled about over it.

What you need to remember
is that
you create your own reality
and your own experience.
All of it.

So whatever you encounter
in or out of meditation
is something you sent out for
and created for yourself.

There is no doubt,
for example,
that you will encounter your fears
somewhere along the way
when you pursue astral explorations.
And that the materialization of them
will come up much more quickly and abruptly
than it will in normal life.

But if you greet any by-products of your fear
with love
instead of with more fear,
they will fade away peacefully
and leave you alone.
Better still,
you will never have to confront them
in your normal life,
where you could actually be hurt by them.
Remember, too,
when you are journeying astrally,
you don't have to worry about your body.

Your body knows how to keep itself safe.
And it will take care of itself
for you.

You maintain an energy connection
automatically
at all times.
And if you sense a problem
like choking
or a fire in the room
or any kind of emergency,
you'll be back in your body at once,
less than an instant after you left it.

No matter how long
it seems like you've stayed away.

The explorations in this section
show you various ways to begin
meditating astrally.
At least one of them can take you
through your conscious barriers.
Wherever you choose to go from there
is limitless
and indescribably miraculous.

Simple astral breakaway

Enter complete meditation
lying down on your back,
noticing how relaxed, heavy and inert
your body feels.

When your inner screen is clear and bright,
visualize your body on it
just as you look when you're lying there.
Get the idea that your body is like
a raincoat you can unbutton
or a scuba wetsuit you can unsnap
and shed at will.
Then visualize the process
of unbuttoning, unsnapping or unzipping
your body
and taking it off.
And let your screen go dim.

When you are ready,
roll over
without using your body.

If you keep your thought-command
and your muscular response separate,
you'll be able to do it
because your muscles in meditation
are so relaxed.

When you roll over,
you'll be looking at yourself.
And as you stand up
or rise weightlessly into the air,
you'll see yourself very clearly.
All of which may shock you
right back into your body.
And cause you to sit up,
fully conscious, sweating, breathing heavily
and wide awake.

At this point,
lie down again and go right back into
complete meditation.

Notice again
how relaxed and heavy and inert
your body is beginning to feel.
And repeat the process:
Visualizing your body
as a raincoat or wetsuit.
Dimming your screen.
And rolling over and out.

Stay out this time
and hover about your room or home
for as long as you like.
When you want to return to your body,
just lie over it and merge into it.
And you'll be back
without any exertion or shock.

You'll know you've projected
out of your body
and that you're not dreaming
or imagining it
by the vividness of what you see.
Astral colors are much brighter
and more sparkling
than colors on the earthbound plane.
And even a drab dull room will look
effervescent and alive.

Unconscious astral breakaway

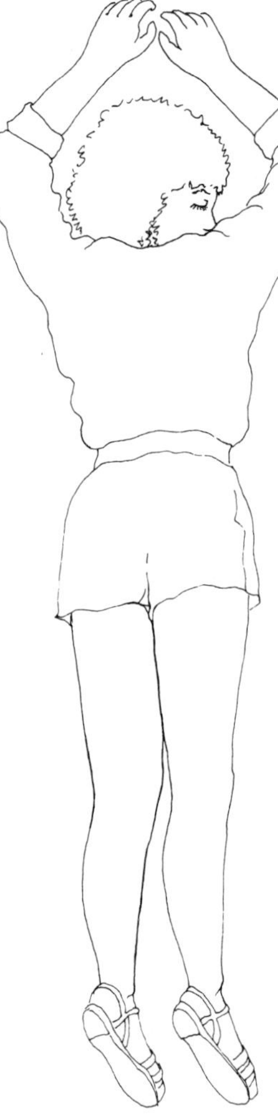

If you experience initial barriers
to astral meditation,
you can still have the end result
without the tension of getting there.
Like this.
Program yourself
during your pre-sleep alpha period.
As you are holding the line
between being awake and being asleep,
tell yourself at least three times:
I will wake myself up
when my astral self is out of my body
and my body will remain asleep.

When you awake,
you will be out of your body
in an altered state of consciousness.
Notice where you are,
how the room and your body look
and how perfectly free you feel.

You can always project your self astrally
this way when you are unconscious
and bring yourself back
to enjoy the experience consciously.

Fine tuning the process

If you still experience astral barriers,
this exploration will empower you
to see exactly where your barrier comes up
and to push beyond it.
After using a compass
to magnetically align your body
to the North,
enter complete meditation
lying on your back.
Relax your body completely
and keep noticing your inner screen
until all the random pictures have cleared.
Then let your screen go dim.

With your eyes closed,
stare at the blackness
on the back of your eyelids
until you lose all contact with
your senses of touch, taste, smell,
hearing and seeing.
When your sensory channels are closed,
you'll begin to feel highly energized
from deep inside yourself
and you'll sense that
all your inner energy is radiating out
like lightlines from a star.

At this point,
begin to notice the lines of energy
that extend through your closed eyelids
and radiate towards the ceiling.
Bring the lines from each eyelid together
between three to six feet above your face.
You'll know when you've found the right spot
because you'll feel some resistance there.

From that spot where your energy lines touch,
bend the beam of energy
from your converged point of contact
into a right angle
so it is focused parallel
with your head and body.
And send a beam outward,
or backward toward the North,
beyond the top of your head
until you reach
a sparking or hissing point of reaction.

Then allow a cone or pyramid to form
from that point
all the way back to your head and body.

You'll begin to vibrate
inside your energy cone as soon as
you've formed it.
Take some time to get used to
the feeling of your vibrations
so that you can recreate it
whenever you want to
later on.

Push your vibrations from the top of your cone
all along the path of your body
and down to your feet.
Let your vibrations engulf you
in what feels like a cross between
a whirlpool and a whirlwind.
And get used to your sensations
at this low-to-medium vibratory level.

Then turn up the juice
and increase the speed of the vibrations
and the vibrational flow all around you.
One push is all you need.
And your vibrations will accelerate
to a higher frequency all on their own.

When your vibratory level is so high
that you begin
to notice a warm tingling feeling
or experience a sudden snap,
you're over the line
and meditating astrally.

Going places

Without the boundaries
of time and space as you know them
to contain you,
the possibilities of astral travel are endless.
And unlike precognition, post cognition
and clairvoyance,
where only one of your senses breaks through,
in out-of-body experiences,
all of you participates
except your body.

The two main destinations are
somewhere or somewhen on earth
and somewhere else.

Earth places have an initial edge
because there is
a certain hominess to them.

You can check out your neighborhood
or your city.
Or go to the mountains or the beach.
Or visit a friend or lover
and see what they are doing.
Or drop in on a childhood adventure
or any other past or future life cycle
you are involved in.

At first,
you'll have a tendency to walk or float or fly
to wherever you are going.
That's fine, but unnecessary.
On the astral level,
all you need to do to get someplace is
to will yourself to be there.
And you'll automatically show up
exactly where you want to be.
Automatically.
And infinitely faster than the speed of light.

Unearthy places are more disorienting.
They include
the far reaches of the galaxies,
the uncharted regions
and dream landscapes of your psyche,
the in-between life and after-life zones
of immortality,
the paths of legends and mythology,
and places where the symbols
and the archetypal essences may be
virtually unrecognizable.

Just keep in mind, you always get somewhere else by willing it.
And you always get back the same way.
Wherever it is,
it's completely up to you.

A short long trip

Enter complete meditation.
If astral separation is easy for you,
roll out or lift out of your body.
If astral separation is difficult,
join in the rest of this exploration anyway,
without it.
Somewhere along the way,
you might just get with it.

From where you are meditating,
project outward
and see what's going on
in the street outside.
Notice the details.
The mailboxes, cars, people, fire hydrants,
trees and bushes.
Notice the sounds, the smells, the activity.
Look even further out
and see what's going on one street away,
two or three streets away
and in the entire area up to
a mile or two away.

Keep expanding outward.
Give yourself enough time
for each level of expansion.
And notice what's going on in your city,
in your state,
in your time zone,
in the whole country.

And keep expanding outward
to include your continent,
your hemisphere
and finally your entire globe.

Then keep going outward
and include space,
the moon,
Venus, Mars and Mercury,
Jupiter and Saturn,
the rest of the solar system,
the milky way,
the galaxy
and finally the universe.
Take it all in.
Enjoy the light show
and all the sounds of all the celestial bodies.
Float and listen and watch and be.

Then,
when you've been long enough,
begin to contract
back toward your center.

Re-view the universe,
the milky way,
the solar system,
the neighboring planets,
the moon,
as you pass by.

Re-view your planet's globe,
your hemisphere,
your continent,
your country, your state, your city,
your neighborhood
and your street.

Contract back into your body.
And notice how good it feels to be back home.
Especially now that you know
you can safely go
as far as you like astrally
in complete meditation.

Reincarnational meditation

Reincarnational meditation

Already you have experienced glimpses
of the truth that
everything that can happen,
that did happen or that will happen,
is happening now.
Altogether and simultaneously.

The reality of that truth exists
whether you are in agreement with it
or not.
You are indeed operating
on more planes and in more lives
than you can imagine.
And by exploring
all of your multi-dimensionality
with an open and adventurous mind
and a child-like playfulness,
you can get to
all the places you are,
all the places you are coming from,
and all the places you are heading for.
In your present lives.
In your past lives.
In your future lives.
And in all the spaces in between.

Traditional reincarntion regression
focuses exclusively on the past.
Which is like saying
you can only travel West
from wherever you are.
And never North, South or East.

Because it is all happening now
on axis points that radiate from you
every moment that you live,

you can reach every place
that your essence touches in time.

You are like the dot
in the center of a cosmic asterisk.
And the lines that intersect
the dot of the moment you are living in
now
can carry you all over time
and back again.

Exploring the past
is an obvious direction to pursue
once you have widened your context
to include reincarnation.
Roots are an issue for everyone.

But at the same time
that you explore your past,
you can also contact other places
where your life force is operational
in the present.
These include:
Other independent lives
in the same or different geographic areas.
And other trace lives
in which all the choices you didn't make
in your life
became energized as choices that got made
in neighboring fields of probability.
These are all the other lines
passing through your cosmic asterisk,
that then became alternative lives.

You can contact these lives very simply
by entering complete meditation
with the question
"Where else am I now?"
formed on your screen.

You'll see where else
in the moments that follow.

Also happening at the same time
as your past
is your future.
And you can reach into it
as easily as you can
reach into the past.
Because the future is constantly connected to
and constantly exerting an influence
on the present.

It works
just as surely as if
the one full grown tree left
in an area cleared for new housing
has made sure that its own seed
was dropped there to grow safely
in the past.

The easiest starting point
is the past.
So for now, you'll want to focus there.
Just keep in mind
that the explorations in this section
extend out from where you are
in every chronological direction.
And you can always apply them
to the present and the future
whenever you wish.

Seeing your reincarnational selves

Enter complete meditation
with a mirror at your side.
Or shift your consciousness to
a near-meditative state,

with your body relaxed
and your breath flowing deeply
in and out of your diaphragm.

When your senses are still,
stare into the mirror.
If your room is dimly lit,
set a flickering candle to one side
of your face.

Stare at the reflection of your eyes
without blinking
for as long as you can,
with the intention of seeing
how you look in other lives.
And watch what happens.

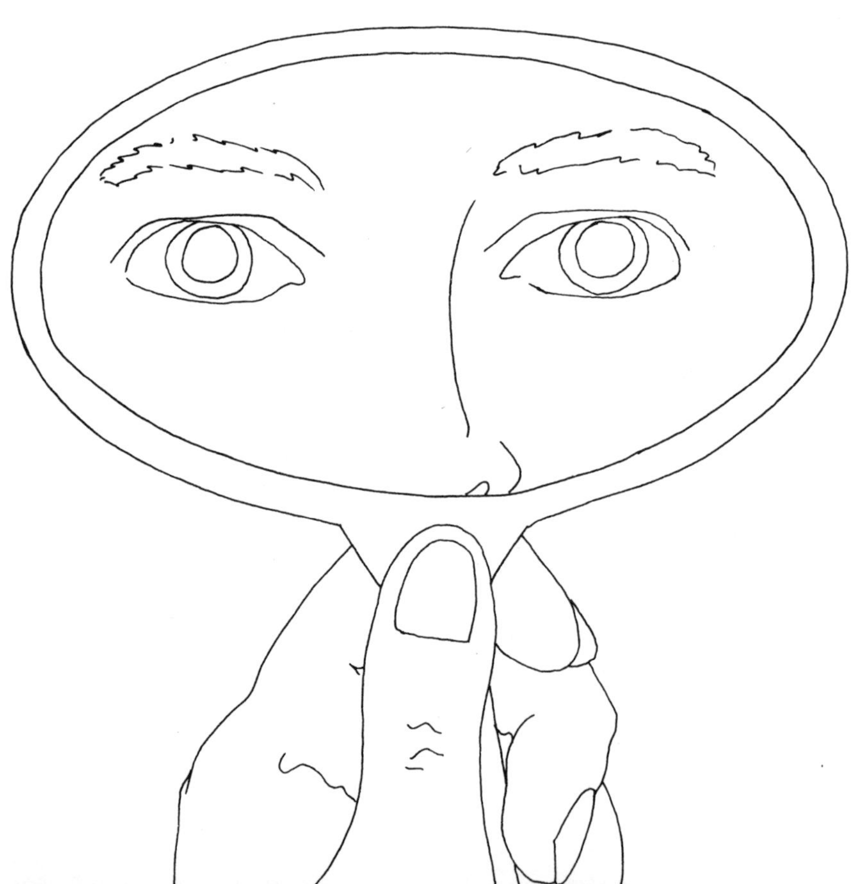

Only your eyes will remain as they are.
Around them,
the rest of your face will shift and melt
and form other characteristics.
You may appear more aged and wrinkled.
And then younger and more attractive.
You may grow a beard and longer hair
or lose the hair you have now.
And you'll probably change your gender
at least once.

Let all the faces and facial features flow
and keep your eyes locked on your eyes
for as long as you can.
You'll see yourself
as others see you in other lives.

More reincarnational seeing

Sit facing someone else.
Any friend, lover, parent or child will do.
Dim the room lights
and light a candle off to one side,
equally spaced between you.

Relax your bodies
and breathe slowly, deeply and rhythmically
together
starring into each other's eyes.
You will experience the same facial changes
you saw in your own face
in the face of your partner.
In additon,
you may notice a change in clothing.
A shirt can turn into a robe or a gown.
Or whatever.
Expect to see a beard grow at least once
and hair lengthen
and a complete change of sexual gender.

In different lives,
you have both male and female experiences.
In this meditation,
you can see that for yourself.

Regression techniques

There are as many ways to regress yourself
into a reincarnational life
as there are reincarnational lives
to regress yourself into.
Most of them involve
extensions of the same techniques
you have been exploring in this book.
Which is why
complete meditation
is a powerful springboard into other lives.

The best regression techniques
involve a combination of
complete toe-to-head body relaxation,
deep and rhythmic diaphragmatic breathing
and a well-developed ability to visualize.

The best regression techniques
also utilize a time-travel device,
after you reach a meditative
or near-alpha state.

You may want to try
the following time-travel mechanisms
by fully visualizing them on your inner screen
and using them at least once.
Then you can pick the one that works best
as your commuter ticket
to other lives.

The tunnel.
You enter a long black tunnel
and you feel your way
along its smooth, worn, well-traveled walls.
After a while,
you see a light way in the distance.
When you reach the light,
you leave the tunnel
and enter another one of your lives.

The bridge.
You are standing on the edge of a chasm.
Across a great distance,
you can see the other side
as if in shadow and mist.
A rainbow forms
joining both sides of the chasm
and you walk across it.
When you reach the other side,
you have reached another lifetime.

The elevator.
You enter an elevator
and notice that according to the floorlights
you are somewhere near the middle.
Since you know you can go
as far up or as far down as you like,
you choose a button
that will take you a few floors down
or back in time.
You press it.
You experience the movement.
And then you reach your destination.
The elevator doors open
and you are on the floor that is
the time-frame of another of your lives.

The digital clock-calendar.
Return to the workspace you created
on page 189,

and notice that the digital clock-calendar
on your desk
can be set in both directions
to any time, day, and year you choose.
Turn the knobs back as far as you like
and watch the numbers on the dial
spin around and change.
When you reach the place in time
where you want to stop,
you can tune in that life
on your television screen and watch it.
Or you can open the door of your workplace
and walk out into it.

Once you are there,
you can adjust the time
and move ahead or behind the year you arrived
in your simultaneous or reincarnational life
to take in the whole experience.
Or you can stay in just one piece of it
for as long as you like.

You may find it easier
to keep a running commentary
of everything that happens.
And even interview your other self
to find out exactly who and where you are.
Or you may just prefer to watch.

Either way,
when you are ready to return,
you can bounce back to your homebase life
instantly.
Or you can return
using the same time-travel device
that took you there.
There is no physical shock involved
and only mild post-meditative

spaceyness
or dissociation.
Going and coming,
the options are endless.
And entirely up to you.

A typical regression

Enter into
complete meditation
in as comfortable
a sitting or lying-down position
as you possibly can.

When you have crossed over into alpha
and your inner screen is clear,
visualize your favorite time-travel device.
And use it.
Say you find the time elevator
easiest to use
and your interest is Renaissance Italy.
Allow two or three buttons per century
and push the one for 1490.

Space is no consideration
when you are time traveling
so it doesn't matter
if you get into your elevator
in Los Angeles or the Bronx.
The doors will open
into the exact part of 15th Century Italy
that you are involved in.

There is a good chance
that you will not be Michelangelo
or Leonardo Da Vinci.
You may find yourself
on a dusty road
leading a mule.

Then again,
you may find yourself
living a princely life in a castle.
Or a merchant or a courtesan.
Or an inquisitor or a nun.

The point is
always take what you get.
Stay with your first image.
And let it be your starting point.

You will probably find yourself
living different lives
in the same century of time.
So be ready to fine-focus
if you get an overlay or bleedthrough.
Whatever period attracts you
definitely has a simultaneous life
going on in it.
And where you have one life,
you usually have several unfolding
at the same time.

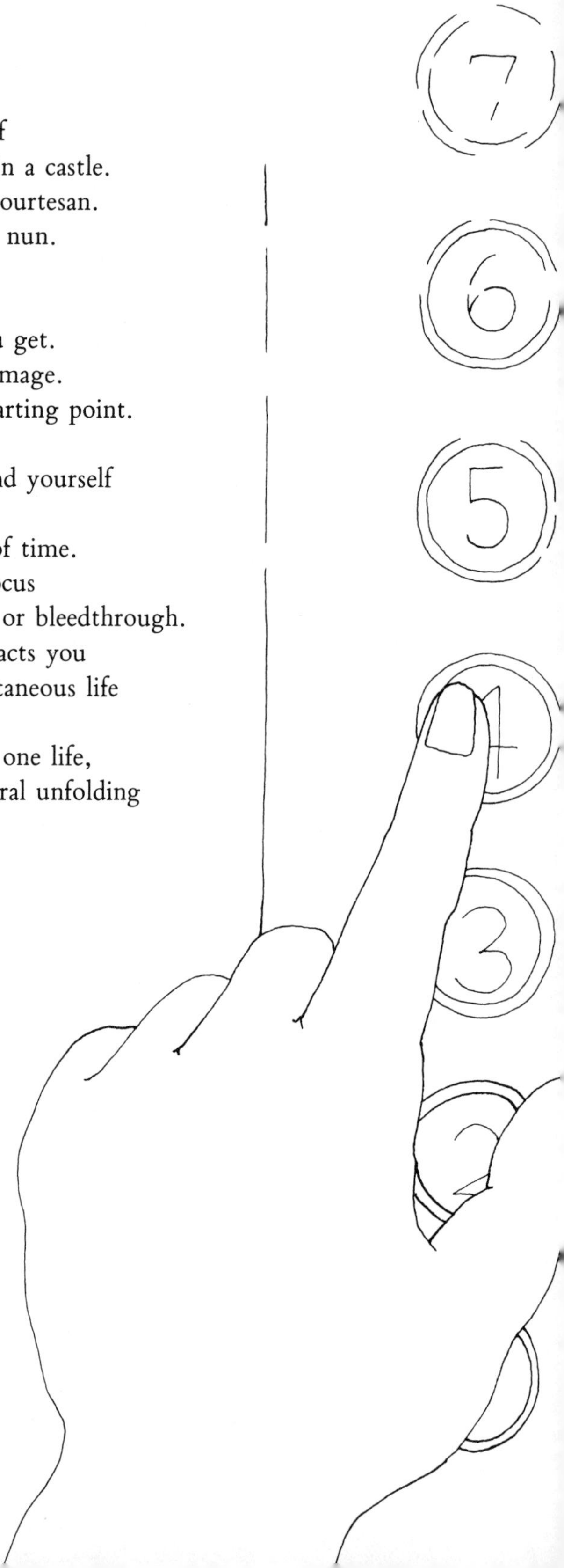

Your energy essence
chooses various times and civilizations
to materialize in
because those are the times that require
your physical presence.
Bleedthroughs are always likely
and very interesting to deal with.
In them,
highly-charged adventure experiences
can be shared with your counterparts.

When your elevator doors open on a scene,
it will be like
zooming in to a close-up shot in a movie.
Let your field of vision widen
and take in as much as you can.
Then move in on your other self again.
And find out who and where you are.

One way to get a name
is to finetune the life you've entered
back to an earlier period
and see what the reincarnative you
was called as a child.

If you come upon yourself
in too emotional a setting
like dying or making love
or having a major crisis,
and you feel scared or uncomfortable,
you can always flashback
to a slightly earlier time and see
what triggered
the event you found yourself in.

It is likely that you will arrive
at crisis points in your other lives.
Because a crisis is so highly charged
with emotion,

it exerts the most powerful force field
and pulls you in most easily.

Pick up as much information as you can
about your life
and your culture at the time of your life.
Many insignificant details can be traced
and substantiated later on.
The name of the province you find yourself in
in Renaisance Italy
may be in an encyclopedia.
And even if you have traveled
to a more distant life
in biblical times or the Atlantean era,
you will probably encounter people
in your present life
who will recall many of the same details
about clothing, technology and cultural problems.

Wander along
in your reincarnational life
for as long as you like.
And notice what emotions come up for you
each step of the way.
If you keep closely in touch
with your feelings,
you can even watch yourself die
in an earlier life
and follow your essence
to a time in between lives.

When you want to return,
either zap back
or reverse your time travel mechanism
by pushing the elevator button
that will return you to your present life.

After you step through the doors
into your own time and your own experience,

continue to relax and breathe deeply
for as long a time as you need
to integrate your journey.
Often at this point,
an insight from your
reincarnational life
can clarify a problem in
your present life.
Be open to these new sources
for understanding yourself.

Then open your eyes.
And write down everything that happened
in a notebook
especially set aside
for reincarnational meditation.

It may seem that you're doing
a lot of notebook work.
But keeping an accurate record
of all your meditational experiences
tends to keep them flowing
more and more easily for you.
And propels you
further and further
beyond your barriers.

Soul meditation

Soul meditation

All of the explorations you've experienced
so far
are meditations
of the body, the mind and the emotions.
Dreams
are meditations of the soul.

Dreams are as close as you can come
to your natural state of beingness.
And in many so-called primitive cultures
and past civilizations
where expanded mental powers
are commonplace,
dream realities are more important
than waking reality.

In dreams,
the multidimensional qualities of your life
become blatently obvious
along with your innate capacity
to create and form objects and events
in the environmental space around you.

As you explore dreams as meditative forms,
two ageless insights
become increasingly clear.
The first is
that all reality is a variation
of the themes of your dreams.
The second is
that we experience open-ended sequences of
dreams within dreams within dreams.

Language is the greatest barrier
to successful dream work.
The deeper into dreams that you go,
the more the language and symbols change.

And while the part of you
that participates in the deepest of dreams
understands all the language and symbols
encountered there,
the rest of you doesn't.
Yet.

Nevertheless,
the symbols you run into in dreams
can be and need to be correlated
with the people, objects and events
that turn up when you are awake,
because they represent
parallel learning and growth experiences
of the highest order.

Begin to get the idea that
dreams are inner places of significant activity
and energy exchange,
much like the shopping centers, cities
or universities of waking life.
Dreams are rallying points
for testing and validating
events, people and choices that
you may or may not materialize
into your physical life
when you are awake.

When the energy for a catastrophic event,
for instance,
is fully expended in a dream,
you never have to create that same event
later on in your waking life.

So you can use your dreams
to encounter and experience
things you are afraid of
and barriers you must still overcome.
With no risks and no losses.

Dream reality is linked to waking reality
in the same way
your soul or spirit is linked to your body.
Dreams are like videotaped takes
or projections of the future
and alternative present events
in the same way that
photographs are like frozen or captured
images of the past.

The soul meditation explorations
of your dream landscapes
in this section
will enable you to begin to
open up the territory.
And to expand your awareness of
how much more there is to you
than you've ever been led to believe.

Recalling your dreams

Before you can consciously work
with your dreams,
you need to become aware of
as much dream content as you can.
So you need to remember your dreams
when you are awake.

Even if you have never remembered a dream
before now,
you can begin to recall
as many as nine a night from now on.

The first few nights,
a small sip of brandy or glass of wine
or a little tea or coffee
or a vitamin B-6 tablet or two
will ease you into remembering your dreams

by strengthening their vividness.
Then, all you need is
a simple nightly programming reminder.

As you drift into alpha,
between waking and sleeping,
affirm to yourself three times:
I will remember my dreams
and wake up and write them down.

Then you need to be ready
to do just that.

Your dream notebook

Keep a notebook or pad of paper,
a pen and a small flashlight
within easy reach of your bed.

When you begin to awaken from a dream,
as you programmed yourself to do,
don't do anything.
Just lie there.
And let all your dream images come to mind
without moving your body at all.
When you have the sequence of your dream
clear in your mind,
sit up and write it down.

The one exception is:
Always write down information
like names, songs, poetry,
or creative ideas
first.
This is really valuable dream
content.
And it is very easy to forget.

You don't have to wake up completely
to write down your dreams.
But whether you do or not,
as you lie down to sleep again,
repeat your affirmation
to remember your dreams, wake up
and write them down.

Sometimes a dream will come to you
later in the day or several days later.
Write it down whenever you get it.
And never let a dream memory slip by
without noticing it and recording it.

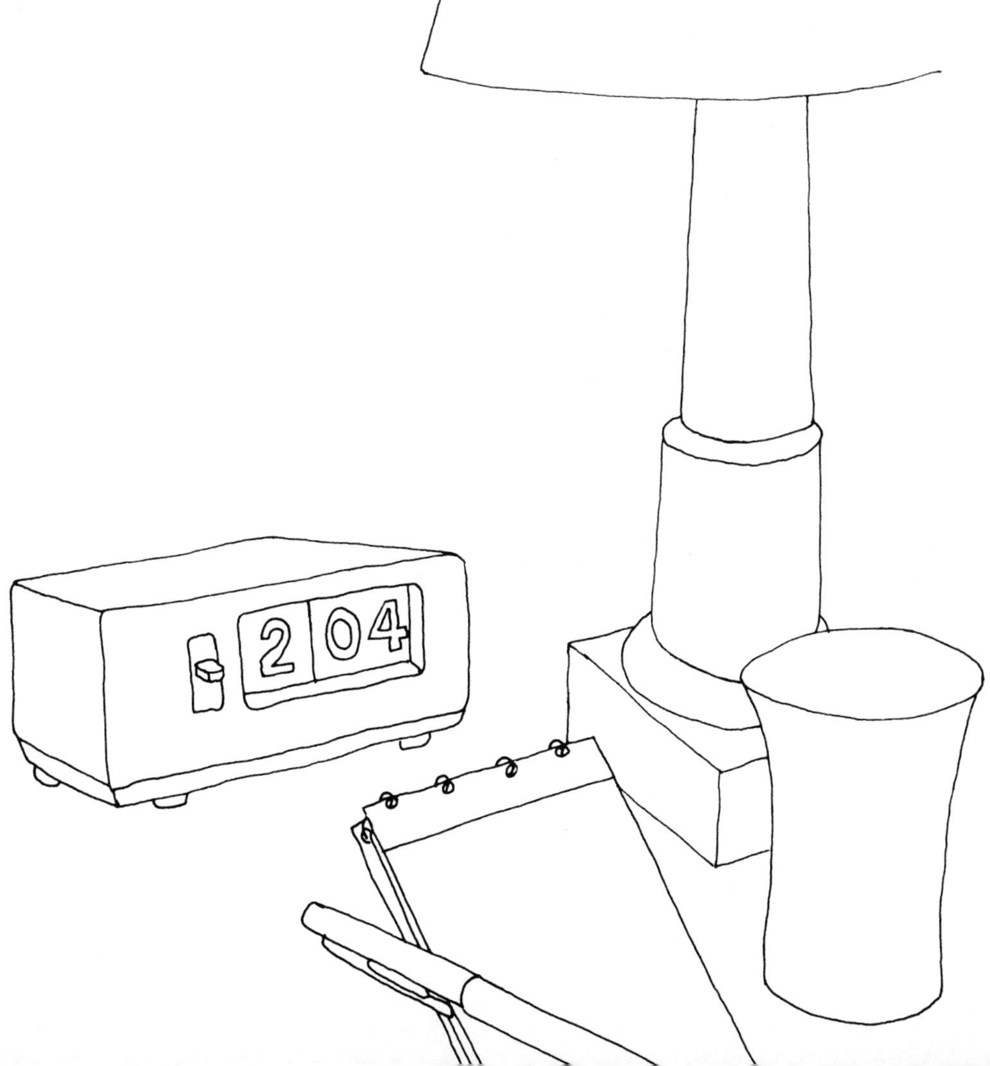

As you get used to recording your dreams,
begin to cultivate a network
of dream friends, acquaintances and lovers
who will support your efforts
and cooperate with your desire to
wake up and write down your dreams
by reminding you to do it
each time a dream begins to fade away.
Once you create your supportive dream team,
dream recording becomes
easy, effortless and almost automatic.

Programming your dreams

Your dreams,
like your waking life,
are much more within your control
than you've ever realized.

And you can easily prove it.
After you have been consistently
recording your dreams for a while,
with no lapses or memory lags,
change your pre-sleep alpha programming
to include
asking for the kind of dream you want.

Create your own programming affirmations
like these:

Tonight, I dream about the answer
to the question
(and insert whatever the question is).

Tonight, my dream restores
my vitality, energy and health.

Tonight, my dream inspires
a new creative idea that will get me
acknowledged.

Always state your affirmation
in the present tense.
And always follow it with the words:
And I will remember it, wake up
and write it down.

Dream expansion techniques

Each of the following short explorations
will expand your capacity
to create dream events of your own choosing.
Play with each one
and see just how far you can take it.

Enter complete meditation.
And on your inner screen, create a dream.
Take the first image you get
and build it into a dream adventure story
or a dream sequence or series of fragments.

When you are finished,
write it down in your dream notebook.

Enter complete meditation.
Get the picture that
an event you have just experienced
in waking life
is a dream.
And that your meditation
is a recreation and continuation
of that dream.

Notice each symbol in your experience.

And see what the people and other elements
really represent.
And what each object or action really means.

Then let a picture
of where you will be when you wake up
from that dream
begin to form on your inner screen.
Imagine that you are waking up in that picture.
And observe all the events that
follow.

When you emerge from
complete meditation,
write your dreams down
in your dream notebook.
And indicate the date and time that
you dreamed them.

Conscious dreaming

As your dream notebook begins to fill up,
you will begin to notice
times when it appears that
you are dreaming about dreaming.
Or times that you dream
you are waking up to record a dream
and that you are really dreaming
the whole time.

When that happens,
you are ready to test and validate
the reality of your dreams
even as you are dreaming them,
by holding your awareness and focus
and letting your dreams unfold
under your direction.
Instead of in fragments or narratives.

You can then bring
anyone or anything you want
into your dream.

You can build your own
settings and cities.
And experiment with what it
would feel like
to indulge your wildest fantasies
and participate in epic dream
adventures.
And do whatever you want with them.

You begin to have the power
of a motion picture director
with unlimited cast, budget,
and locations
to choose from.

One way to become a conscious presence
in your dreams
is to tell yourself
that you will pretend you are awake
when you are asleep.
And that
instead of sleeping,
you will merely enter another dimension
of being awake.

Another way is to
learn to become sensitized
to the sensations that occur
on bodily and emotional levels
whenever dreams begin, run through, and end.
And to imagine as you sensitize yourself
that you are fully awake
and fully participating in the action.

Pay attention to any incongruities
with your waking reality.
And watch for unusual phenomena.
When a person or object
changes its size, solidness or shape,
acknowledge that it means
you must be dreaming.
When you notice yourself flying
or dreaming that you are awake,
you can quickly step in
and begin to exercise your conscious control.

Conscious dreaming is an advanced yogic skill.
As you practice it,
you empower an incredible connection
between your waking and sleeping modes,
and allow the limitations of
your day-night dichotomy
to fade away into nothingness.

Dream space

When you dream
you are in a room or a building,
extend the field of context
to include the street, town or community
that surrounds your dream location.

Widening the space of your dream landscape
strengthens your ability
to create and materialize experience.
And brings you closer to
the point of contact
with your waking reality.
Using the same psychic muscles,
you can begin to widen the space
of your waking life
to include more and more of what you want.

Dream time

When you notice that you are dreaming,
expand the time frame of your dream scene.
Like videotape,
run the scene backward
by telling yourself you want to know
what happened before you tuned in
to your dream.

The past will flow
out of any moment you will it
to flow from,
just as the future does
with no stopping points along the way.

Dream time
can be speeded up or slowed down,
run back to an origin point
or a new beginning
or ahead to any of hundreds
of probable outcomes.
Waking time works exactly the same way.
And practicing in your dreams
enables you
to break through artificial time barriers
that have been limiting
your effectiveness in your waking life.

Moment meditation

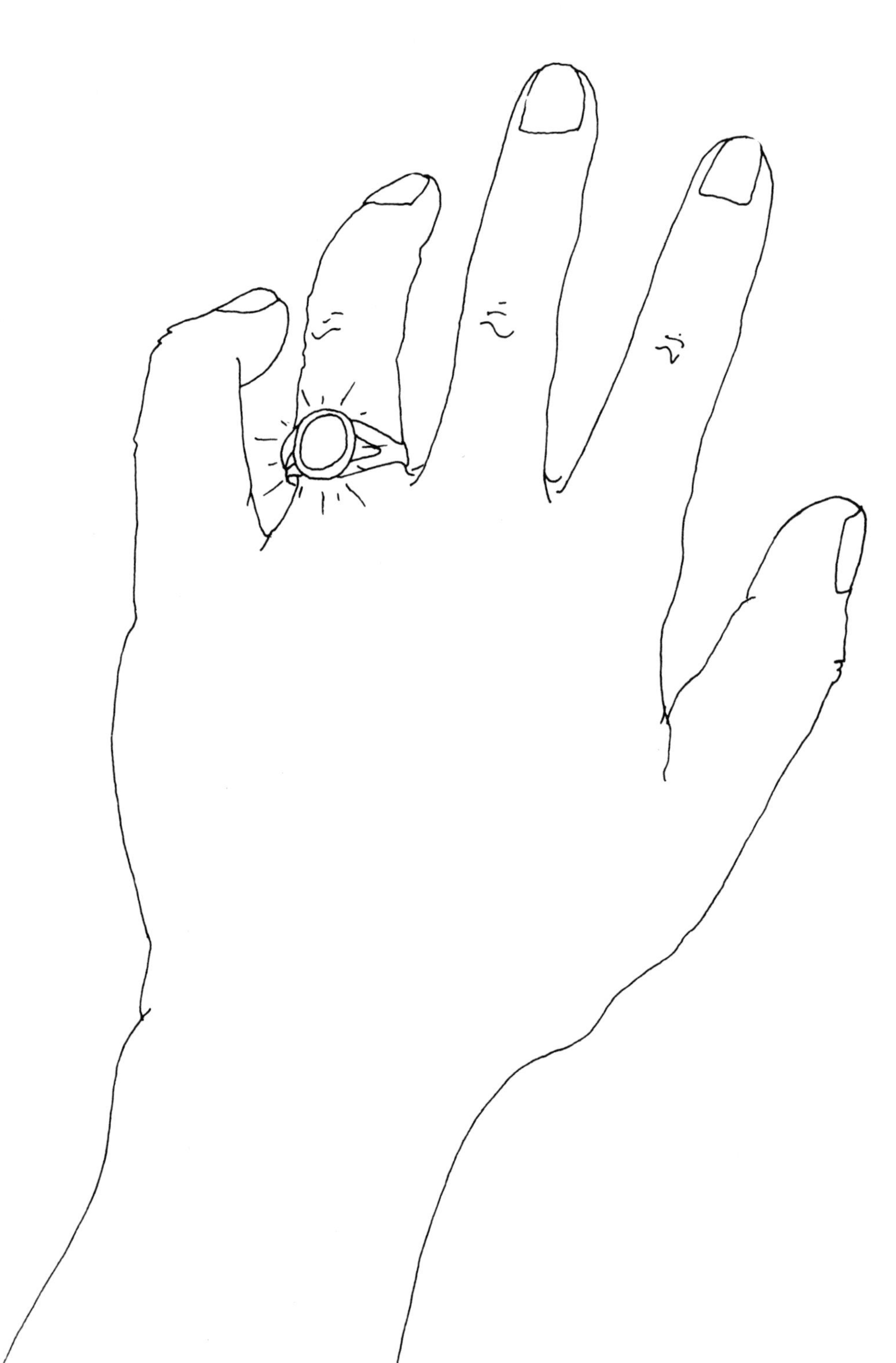

Moment meditation

By now,
your awareness about
and your connections into
complete meditation
are forged strongly enough
to make many of the preliminaries
unnecessary.

And whenever you wish,
you can begin to lower yourself
into an alpha or near-alpha state.
Even if you only remain there
for a few seconds at a time,
you can emerge refreshed and relaxed
because meditative time flows
at such a radically different rate.

The explorations in this section
will work for you
whenever you have a moment or two
to shift your consciousness
into complete mediation.

Your ring

Inhale deeply
and join the tip of your thumb
with the tips of the first two fingers
of your right hand.

As you exhale slowly,
focus your gaze on your ring
or any piece of jewelry.
Stare at whichever highlight happens
to catch your eye.

A spot

Inhale deeply
and connect your thumb
with the tips of the first two fingers
of your right hand.

As you exhale slowly,
allow your eyes to focus
on the first spot you notice
on the floor, wall or ceiling nearest you.
Stay with it for a moment.

The stoplight

When you stop for a red light,
stare at the redness
with both eyes.
And breathe as many long deep breaths
in and out
as you can
before the traffic light
changes back to green.

Your chakra

Choose the quality of life
you need more of,
whenever you notice an unfulfilled need.
Then hook up with the chakra
that provides it.

For instance,
if you are in a low
and need some extra energy,
inhale deeply.

Join your thumb
and the first two fingertips
of your right hand
together.
And,
as you exhale slowly,
tune into your solar chakra
(shown in the diagram on page 138)
and softly hum its sound.
Whatever sound you get will be right.

No matter what you need in your life,
your chakras can provide you
with the right quality of energy
to get it.

Instant relief

When you experience a sudden pain
or the recurrence
of a persistent problem,
focus on the part that is irritating you.
Join your thumb and first two fingertips
of your right hand
together.
And inhale deeply into the painful spot.
As you exhale,
allow the pain to be carried away
on your breath.

More instant relief

As a variation,
focus on the chakra
that's nearest to the pain you feel.
Join the thumb and first two fingertips
of your right hand
together.

And inhale into the chakra.
As you exhale,
hum a soft OM on the right chakral note
and send the chakra's power
radiating through your body.
It will vaporize your soreness and pain
in just one or two breaths.

Countdown

Inhale deeply.
Join your thumb
and first two fingertips.
And as you exhale slowly,
count backwards
from ten to zero.
Visualize each number clearly
on your inner screen.
Notice the instantaneous feeling
of calmness spreading over you.

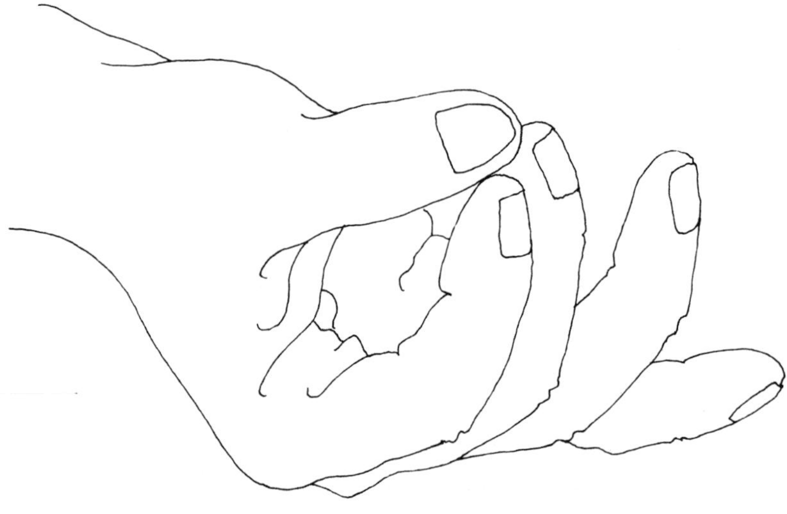

Your portable pyramid

Tune in
to the feelings and sensations
in the space at the back of your skull,
just above the point
where your head joins your neck.

From the feelings you perceive there,
no matter how dim,
allow a pyramid shape to form
as you breathe deeply and rhythmically.

The top of the pyramid will project upwards
above your head.
And the sides will extend down
all around you
from that point.
Your pyramid may be solid
or it may appear to be made of light.

Once you have it working for you,
your pyramid is a vehicle
that can transport your consciousness
to any place or time
in your own multidimensionality
that you wish to visit or see.
You may use it to travel.
Or to simply recharge yourself
on the spot.

The space between

Wherever you are,
look up at any object across the room
that has a relatively clear space
between it and you.

Focus your eyes on that object
as you inhale deeply.
And as you exhale slowly,
shift your focus
to the space between you and the object.

Focus on the emptiness of the space
as you continue to breathe rhythmically.
Allow yourself to be surprised
when you begin to perceive
the other things and life forms
that occupy that space.
and appear
first as shadows,
then in more and more solid form.

Once you begin to expand and redefine
your sensory data,
you begin to realize
that emptiness for you is actually
fullness for what's not you.

Observing how you share space
with other multidimensional life
enables your own consciousness
to stretch its muscles and expand to include
new paths of awareness.

The past

As you inhale,
reach for the first remembered scene
from the past
that comes to your mind.

Then extend it.
By allowing its future
to unfold on your inner screen.

It doesn't matter
whether the future unfolds
as you remember it historically
or not.

The future you see
projecting from your past event
is the future version of the event
that you are now actually creating
and materializing
on some other probable or possible plane
of reality.
And as you can see,
creativity of that magnitude
can occur in the briefest of moments.

The future

Take any event
you experienced today.
And on your inner screen,
allow any one probable outcome
of that event
to emerge and project into the future.

Unfreezing images

Take any photograph of yourself
out of your scrapbook
and stare at it.

Allow the image of the person
you are looking at
to project into the present moment.
And notice whether or not the image
is still you.

Or if it is some past version of you
that has gone into another future
than the one that you are now in.
If you are not still the person
in the photograph,
in your next complete meditation
see whether you can discover
where that other person has gone.

Alternative paths of reality

Begin to get the picture
that the moment you are now experiencing
is one point
on a straight-line path
of conscious awareness.
And that crossing that point
is a matrix of other straight-line paths
of conscious awareness
like the arms of an asterisk.

All the arms of the asterisk
intersect.
Right at the moment-point where you are
right now.

When you get that picture clearly,
inhale.
And as you exhale,
shift off your straight-line path
on to one of the other straight-line paths
that converge at your point.
And follow the alternate path
of alternate consciousness
on your inner screen.

The more you explore
these alternate straight-line paths
of consciousness,
the better you get to know the certainty
of your nature as
a multidimensional being.
And each time you explore it,
it only takes a moment.

Living meditation

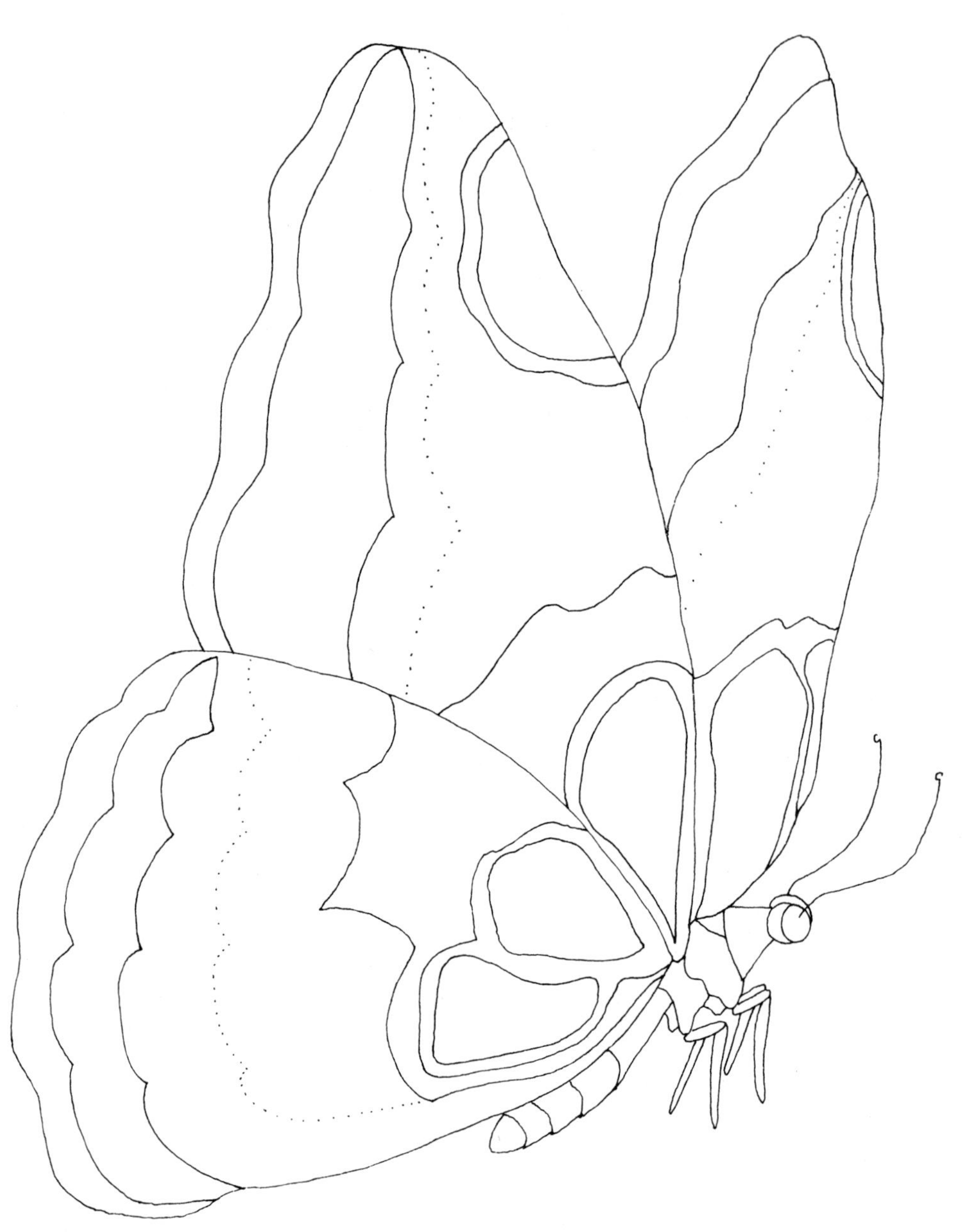

Living meditation

As you work and play with
the explorations you have been reading,
you will find that your over-all approach
to living with
and with-in
yourself
can become more expansive,
less fearful
more open to things as they really are
instead of things as someone told you
they really were.

You will become more and more stable
to guide your own life
and to handle the effects
of time, space and other people
on your life.

You will begin to experience
a feeling of certainty
that no one has more answers
than you do.
And that no one has less.
You'll begin to notice
that people around you are less
different from you
than they used to be.
And that your sensations
of knowing what you know
are stronger than ever before.

Those sensations of inner
confidence and peace
will continue
as you continue exploring meditations
that keep you in touch with

all the power and creativity
you have at your source
and at your command.

Don't hold back.
Experiment.
You will never encounter anything
fearful or threatening
that you have not created yourself
from your own experience.
And whatever you create,
you can choose to dissolve or keep.
As long as you accept it and love it,
the choice is always yours.

So try everything you've read
at least once.

And make a note
of which explorations work best now.
And which ones may work best
some other time.

Remember,
you are dealing with ideas that focus you
inwardly with great intensity.
And that you will be blasting barriers
right and left.
And that when you are done,
you will have gotten back
to being yourself as you were
before you were five years old.
Before you bought the cultural lies
that made you less than you are.
Before you locked up your power
to create and materialize
the substance, events, and reality
of your life.

So along the way,
one by one
you will open your chakral energy vortices
and recapture your innate capacity for life.
As your lower chakras unfold,
you will experience incredible surges
of natural vitality.
As your higher chakras awaken,
you'll discover your spirituality
and psychic gifts.
In between
as you connect with your heart chakra,
you'll find everything you touch
turning to love.

All these things won't happen
all the time.
But you'll find them happening
often enough
to know that you are
definitely on your way.
And what you will reach
with what you will rediscover in this book
over and over and over again,
if you are really open to it,
is the state that mystics call
enlightenment.

You'll find enlightenment
fluttering in a field of love
like a butterfly.
Fragile.
Incredibly beautiful.
Brightly colored.
Elusive.
You'll touch it and pull back.
And touch it again,
only to see it fly beyond your reach.
And touch it again,
attempting to hold it.

Soon,
you'll grasp the paradox.
You'll find enlightenment and love inside yourself.
But the only way to hold onto them
is by sharing them,
outside of yourself.

So,
as your power expands,
get out and expand your circle of participation
in the world you are creating
around yourself.
Tell people you meet
about your meditative adventures.
You may feel shy in the beginning.
But as you share yourself,
everyone you talk to
will either
draw closer in fascination
or pull back in fear of your
expansiveness and openness
and willingness to love and be loved.
Which makes it easy for you to figure out
who you want to include in your life.

As you begin to realize
that everyone in the universe
has the power
to expand their lives as you are doing,
it will matter less and less
how you are perceived, judged or evaluated.

What is, is.
And what you experience, is your experience.
Regardless of anyone else's
considerations about it.
Sharing yourself
openly, honestly, and recklessly
with the lives and events you touch
will feed your newfound enlightenment,

strengthen it and solidify it
for you.

You began your journey into
complete meditation
by turning completely inward.
You'll keep all the treasures you find there
by turning them out
warmly and lovingly
and making room for more.

Keep living in
complete meditation.
Just one short trip a day
will maintain your connections
with everything you need to know
about everything you'll ever need to know
to let yourself be
simply and completely
yourself.

Index

Afterword

Afterword

When I was a little boy, I used to sit out under the stars from time to time on summer nights and lose myself in the vastness I had created all around me.

Years later, I found out that was called meditating. Norma, my first love and wife at that time, got me to go to a TM lecture with her. The payoff was, they said for some money they'd show me how it worked. It looked so good I would probably have paid them. But when I saw the demonstration, I knew I knew how already.

It's been that way ever since.

I went from my own version of TM, complete with changing mantras to match my changing levels of awareness, to my own versions of each of the other areas of meditation in this book.

Each time I thought I needed to learn something new, I found out I already knew it. I just didn't know I knew. Until I started doing it.

Two spectacular meditative moments stand out.

One happened during a bathtub meditation. I noticed a large lynx-sized Egyptian cat wrapped around the toilet and I began to get pictures of circles with strange symbols written all over them, and ongoing tables of other old symbols, numbers and other data. I wrote down as much as I could remember. And one of the things I ended up with was a close approximation of my own natal astrology chart.

Later I found out that from out of nowhere and with absolutely no interest in the subject, I had picked up a definitive knowledge of serious astrology. And in subsequent meditations, the whole ancient science came through clearly. I even got some stuff I don't know how to use yet, mixed in with what I now apply all the time in my day-to-day life.

Just as incredible were my early out-of-body meditations in which I discovered how to use my inner passport to everywhere that is and was and ever will be.

And then, there's all the rest of it. The chakras opening up, healing that worked, creating dynamic changes all around me, and finally being able to share my love and my vitality on ever-deepending levels. I still don't understand it all, and I know I don't have to understand it to be enriched by it.

One of my publisher's people wanted me to do a bibliography. I couldn't. Because practically everything in this book has come out of my own meditating. I wrote the outline. And one by one, each chapter just sort of appeared.

As my inner sources made this book so readily available and easily communicable to everyone, I began to realize that all of this information has been coming through for years. And the only differences are in the openness, the communication skills and the belief systems of each person who receives the material.

For instance, I want to acknowledge a lot of what I've read and enjoyed in books by Jane Roberts, Richard Bach and Brugh Joy for confirming my own explorations and my sense of what I already knew. I also acknowledge Werner Erhard and The est Training for an experience that led to my conclusion that everyone can meditate. In fact, it was during my own training when I and some 280 other folk traveled together into rocks and daisies that I finally stopped thinking that meditation and consciousness projection were something different and only for the elite.

In addition, for their insights into key parts of the religious meditation chapter, I thank my friends Father Charlie Flaherty and Father John Hall.

Finally, my sincere appreciation goes out to some 3000 centuries or more of meditators, medicine men, messiahs, prophets and spiritual guides without whose help, encouragement and sharing this book could never have been written.

Appendix

Use this exploration from my book
Complete Relaxation
whenever physical tension blocks your meditations.

Your complete relaxation cycle

Lie down on your back
on a comfortable mat.
Or sit in a comfortable chair
with your feet flat on the floor.
Spread your legs slightly apart.
And let your hands fall at your sides,
palms up.

Breathe your basic relaxation breath.
Close your eyes.
And send your awareness
down to your feet.
Tense your feet
by tightly curling your toes.

Inhale. And hold.
As you exhale,
relax your toes and send the tension away.

Tense the backs of your legs
by straightening your feet
and moving your toes toward your face.

Inhale. And hold.
As you exhale,
relax your legs and let all the tension go.

Tense your thighs
by straightening your legs and locking your knees
and lifting them about two inches
off the floor.

Inhale. And hold.
As you exhale,
drop your legs.
And let all the tension drain out of them.

Breathe your basic relaxation breath.
And as you exhale,
forget your feet and legs and thighs
altogether.

Let your awareness drift
to your hips and buttocks and genitals
and internal organs.

Tighten your buttocks and lift them.
Inhale. And hold.

As you exhale,
relax your buttocks and let them drop,
drained of all tension.

Breathe your basic relaxation breath.
If you notice any tension from your waist down,
as you exhale,
send it all away.
And notice how completely relaxed
you are becoming.

Let your awareness
flow into your hands and arms.
Stretch your fingers out,
raising the center of your palms.
Hold for one complete breath.
Inhaling. And exhaling.

Then make fists and tense and clench.
Straighten your arms and fists
about two inches away from your body.

Inhale. And hold.
Tighten your forearms and upper arms.

As you exhale,
let your arms drop.
And let your hands fall,
palms up,
like gloves lying on a table, empty and still.
Completely relaxed.

Shrug your shoulders
and try to push them up to your ears.
Inhale. And hold.

As you exhale,
let your shoulders drop.
And feel how relaxed they are.
Allow your awareness to flow
into your back.
Arch your spine up
toward the sky.
Inhale. And hold.

As you exhale,
let your spine melt into your mat or chair.
And sense the relaxation
flowing through your back.

Tighten your chest and stomach.
Draw each muscle in and tense it.
Inhale. And hold.

As you exhale,
let each muscle go loose and limp.
And feel the soothing calmness flow in.

Breathe your basic relaxation breath.
And feel how completely relaxed you are
from the neck down.

Roll your head gently
from side to side.
And feel how relaxed your neck is becoming.
Breathe your basic relaxation breath.
And if you can find
any tension anywhere in your body,
when you exhale
send it all away.
And forget that you even have a body.

Let your awareness drift into your face.
Press your tongue
against the roof of your mouth,
tighten your jaw muscles
and clench your teeth.
Inhale. And hold.

As you exhale,
open your mouth wide
and yawn for a moment,
then let your mouth be.

Feel how peaceful you are,
as your lips separate slightly
and your chin relaxes completely.

Now wrinkle your nose,
mash your lips against it,
tighten your forehead,
and make ugly prune faces.
Inhale. And hold.
As you exhale,
enjoy the tingling feeling of dissolving tension
all through your face.

Now you are feeling loose
and completely relaxed.

Lie still.
And let your breathing become
deeper and deeper.

With every inhalation,
you breathe new life and vitality
into your body.

With every exhalation,
you breathe old residual tensions
out of your body.

When you allow yourself
to become this completely relaxed,
the process becomes automatic.
You don't have to do anything
but lie where you are.

And feel free.

If you sense the beginning
of tension anywhere,
just deepen your basic relaxation breath.
And send it to that place.

Fill it with breath.
And let your exhalation
carry all the tension away.

Lie where you are
for as long as you want,
feeling better than you have ever felt
before.

And think to yourself:
"I can return here
to this sanctuary of complete relaxation

whenever I wish,
simply by joining my thumb
and first two fingertips
of each hand
together like this,
inhaling my basic relaxation breath one time,
and on the exhalation,
saying to myself:
'Relax. . . Relax. . . Relax. . .' "

Now you have programmed the Relaxation Reflex
when you are fully receptive and responsive.
To activate it later,
all you have to do is inhale.

With your eyes open or closed,
join your thumb and first two fingers
and recall the effect of your relaxation cycle,
exploring your body from your toes to your head.
As you exhale,
say to yourself:
"Relax. . . Relax. . . Relax. . . "
And sense all the tension leaving you.

When you are completely relaxed
and ready to return
count backward to yourself
from ten to one.

Your energy will return
at its own rate.
Starting in your toes and fingertips
and spreading
throughout your body.

At the count of one,
you will feel completely rested,
completely alert,
and completely relaxed.

photo by John Goldie

Steve Kravette is a freelance writer who lives in Cohasset, Massachusetts. He is the author of a previous book, *Complete Relaxation*. He is currently teaching a course in relaxation and awareness, serving as a creative consultant for a variety of advertising clients and is working on two new books.

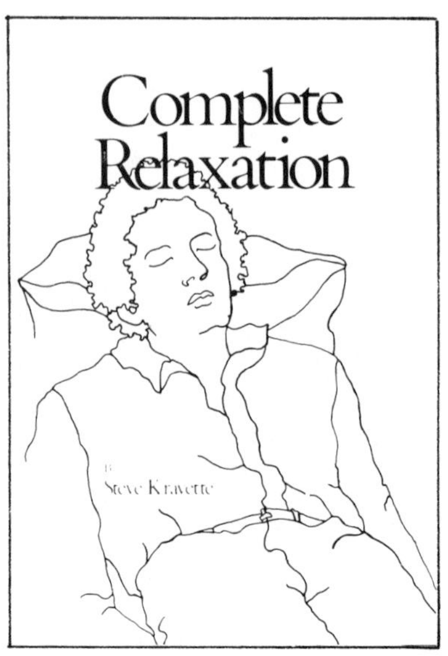

COMPLETE RELAXATION

Steve Kravette

Complete Relaxation is unique in its field because, unlike most relaxation books, it takes a completely relaxed approach to its subject. You will find a series of poetic explorations interspersed with text and beautifully drawn illustrations designed to put you in closer touch with yourself and the people around you. *Complete Relaxation* is written for all of you: your body, your mind, your emotions, your spirituality, your sexuality—the whole person you are and are meant to be.

As you read this book, you will begin to feel yourself entering a way of life more completely relaxed than you ever thought possible. Reviewer Ben Reuven stated in the *Los Angeles Times*, "*Complete Relaxation* came along at just the right time—I read it, tried it; it works."

Some of the many areas that the author touches upon are: becoming aware, instant relaxation, stretching, hatha yoga, Arica, bioenergetics, Tai chi, dancing, and the Relaxation Reflex.

Mantras, meditating, emotional relaxation, holding back and letting go, learning to accept yourself, business relaxation, driving relaxation .

Family relaxation, nutritional relaxation, spiritual relaxation, sensual relaxation, massage and sexual relaxation. *Complete Relaxation* is a book the world has been tensely, nervously, anxiously waiting for. Here it is. Read it and relax.

ISBN 0-914918-14-1
320 pages, 6½" x 9¼", paper $8.95

Books from Para Research

DEVELOP YOUR PSYCHIC SKILLS

by Enid Hoffman

The author's long experience with psychic phenomena is integrated with the practical implications of recent brain research showing how we all have psychic abilities waiting to be developed. The book includes excercises for training both perceptive and projective skills, for clearing obstructing beliefs, for past life recall and many more experiences now available to all who would develop their potential psychic powers. The author says, "I have always felt it important for my students to understand how natural and human a process it is to develop one's psychic skills." She also makes it a lot of fun. Paper, $7.95.

NUMEROLOGY AND THE DIVINE TRIANGLE

by Faith Javane & Dusty Bunker

At last a truly comprehensive and authoritative text on numerology! *Numerology and the Divine Triangle* embodies the life work of Faith Javane, one of America's most respected writers and teachers of numerology, and her student and co-author, Dusty Bunker, a teacher and columnist on metaphysical topics.

Part I is a complete introduction to esoteric numerology and includes a section on the life of Edgar Cayce as a case study of numerology in action.

Part II includes extensive delineations of each of the numbers 1 to 78 and, for the first time in book form, a synthesis of numerology, astrology and the Tarot. Each of the Tarot cards is illustrated. *Numerology and the Divine Triangle* is number one in its field, the book to which all books on the subject will be compared from now on. Paper, $10.95.

NUMEROLOGY AND YOUR FUTURE

by Dusty Bunker

In her second book, Dusty Bunker stresses the predictive side of numerology. Personal periods, including yearly, monthly and even daily cycles, are explored as the author presents new techniques for revealing future developments. The numerological significance of decades is analysed with emphasis on the particular importance of the 1980's. Looking toward the future, the author presents a series of examples from the past, particularly the historical order of American presidents in relation to keys from the Tarot, to illustrate the power of numbers. This book is for everyone; it is easy, instructive and fun to read. Illustrated. Paper, $9.95.

PLANETS IN ASPECT: Understanding Your Inner Dynamics

by Robert Pelletier

Explores aspects, the planetary relationships that describe our individual energy patterns, and how we can integrate them into our lives. Undoubtedly the most thorough in-depth study of planetary aspects ever published. Every major aspect—conjunction, sextile, square, trine, opposition and inconjunct—is covered: 314 aspects in all. Paper, $12.95.

PLANETS IN COMPOSITE: Analyzing Human Relationships
by Robert Hand

The definitive work on the astrology of human relationships. Explains the technique of the composite chart, combining two individuals' charts to create a third chart of the relationship itself, and how to interpret it. Case studies plus twelve chapters of delineations of composite Sun, Moon and planets in all houses and major aspects. Paper, $13.95.

PLANETS IN HOUSES: Experiencing Your Environment
by Robert Pelletier

Brings the ancient art of natal horoscope interpretation into a new era of accuracy, concreteness and richness of detail. Pelletier delineates the meaning of each planet as derived by counting from each of the twelve houses and in relation to the other houses with which it forms trines, sextiles, squares and oppositions, inconjuncts and semisextiles. Seventeen different house relationships delineated for each planet in each house, 2184 delineations in all! Paper, $12.95.

PLANETS IN LOVE: Exploring Your Emotional and Sexual Needs
by John Townley

The first astrology book to take an unabashed look at human sexuality and the different kinds of relationships that people form to meet their various emotional and sexual needs. An intimate astrological analysis of sex and love, with 550 interpretations of each planet in every possible sign, house and aspect. Discusses sexual behavior according to mental, emotional and spiritual areas of development. Cloth, $12.95.

PLANETS IN TRANSIT: Life Cycles for Living
by Robert Hand

A psychological approach to astrological prediction. Delineations of the Sun, Moon and each planet transiting each natal house and forming each aspect to the natal Sun, Moon, planets, Ascendant and Midheaven. The definitive book on transits. Includes introductory chapters on the theory and applications of transits. Paper, $18.95.

PLANETS IN YOUTH: Patterns of Early Development
by Robert Hand

A major astrological thinker looks at children and childhood. Parents can use it to help their children cope with the complexities of growing up, and readers of all ages can use it to understand themselves and their own patterns of early development. Introductory chapters discuss parent-child relationships and planetary energies in children's charts. All important horoscope factors delineated stressing possibilities rather than certainties. Paper, $13.95.

Complete Meditation

Anyone can meditate.
Including you.
It's no secret science
or mystical esoteric process,

All it takes
is a little commitment.
a little practice,
a little development
and this book,
to learn to use this timeless and proven tool
for self-expansion and personal growth from within.

To meditate,
you really don't have to learn to do anything.
You simply have to be.
In fact, the whole idea of Complete Meditation
is to stop doing whatever you are already doing,
and focus completely
on the subject of your meditation.

Whether you've meditated before or not,
this is the book that simplifies all the techniques,
from the easiest to the most advanced.
It's the book that removes the blocks
while dissolving resistance and obstacles,
making meditation the most natural thing in the world.
This is Complete Meditation.
And you have already begun.

By Steve Kravette

ISBN 0-914918-28-1
Psychology, Meditation, Occult

$9.95